COUNTRY COLLECTION

Lyn Smart

a book of country food and facts
with over 200 potato recipes

Go, little book, and wish to all
Flowers in the garden, meat in
    the hall,
A bin of wine, a spice of wit,
A house with lawns enclosing it,
A living river by the door,
A nightingale in the sycamore!

R.L.Stevenson

**Published by Spectator Publications Limited
for the Potato Marketing Board**

COUNTRY COLLECTION was
edited and designed by
Spectator Publications Limited,
91 St Martin's Lane, London WC2H 0DN
for the Potato Marketing Board
50 Hans Crescent, London SW1X 0NB
© Spectator Publications Limited 1977
Recipes © Potato Marketing Board 1977

Photographs on pages 4-16 inclusive
by Bryce Attwell

Illustrations on pages 48, 57, 78,
86, 89, 90 and 111 by Jane Scott

Filmsetting by Citype Limited
Leicester LE4 6AW, Leicestershire

Printed and bound by
Hunt Barnard Web Offset Limited
Aylesbury, Buckinghamshire

Third Impression 1978
ISBN 90086934 8

Introduction

I like to think this book came about because of a childhood game I used to play up in the Pentland Hills near my father's farm. Wandering up there of a summer's Sunday with one or more of my sisters, I would look down on the countryside spread out below like a patchwork quilt - the essence of British countryside in a sweep of the eye. My artistic sister would try to paint it. But not me. Mine was the cook's eye view of the country. I would turn all the crops into dishes. I even made up grassy recipes for the cows! On my return, my Mother, teasing, would say 'Well, Lyn, what recipes have you brought home from your cook's tour today?'.

By the time this book was a twinkle in the Potato Marketing Board's eye, I had accumulated a whole collection of country recipes which, later, travelling round the country as a cookery demonstrator just grew and grew.

Keeping pace in bulginess with my recipe collection was my scrapbook - photographs and drawings, snippets of favourite poetry and prose and lots of odds and ends! Here, a selection of them provides a background for my recipes.

I had three very firm ideas in my mind when making my selection of recipes for this book, for I wanted it to be the *first* cookbook you would turn to on your shelf for inspiration and information. Firstly, the products mentioned should be readily available. Secondly, the method of preparation should be written down in such a way that you wouldn't have to grope around looking for each bit of the recipe. Thirdly, no recipe would be the sort requiring a lot of fiddling and fuss. So this is essentially a practical cookery book and the recipes are all for wholesome, tasty, easily made dishes, for, let's face it, this is what most families prefer. For slap-up occasions, most of us keep a Robert Carrier somewhere on the bookshelf, or we can pop out to the local French or Italian Restaurant. Though for those of you who like entertaining at home, I have included just one or two glamorous recipes.

All the recipes in this collection contain potatoes. I was a potato fan long before I worked for the Potato Marketing Board. I use cooked potatoes as often as I use flour for thickening soups and stews (they never go lumpy!) and for all kinds of quick dishes when people drop in suddenly. Rather like classic clothes, potatoes can, as you will discover in this book, be dressed up or down for different occasions.

I shall now give you in words and pictures a taster of some of the dishes you will find in my Country Collection. But before you turn the page, I would like to say thank you to those of you who have given or sent me potato recipes. From an excellent selection, I have chosen the following for inclusion in my book: Potato and Bacon Cakes; Potato and Herring Savoury Salad - Mrs. E. Hughes, Eglwysbach, Colwyn Bay: Cheese and Potato Sticks - Mrs. P. A. Suggitt, Brandsby, Yorkshire: Children's Favourite Potato and Cheese Pie - Mrs. M. Swiner, Marston, Bedfordshire: Salmon Soufflé; Golden Tripe Fritters - Mrs. I. Green, Compton Dundon, Somerset: Potato Doughnuts - Mrs. R. Blackhall, Durris, Aberdeenshire.

Lyn Smart

Starting with vegetables, Britain's primary food in my opinion and to which, thank Heaven, we are now returning with more enthusiasm because, cooked properly, we are discovering not only their health giving qualities, but how delicious they can be, even used on their own as a substitute for expensive fish and meat.

Most of the vegetables in this photograph have just been freshly dug and cut. One of the bonus' of owning a vegetable garden or allotment is that you can eat vegetables straight from the ground! But flavour, colour and vitamins can still be preserved with shop bought vegetables by cooking them slowly with the minimum of water, or, like the Chinese, by the stir-fry method: Put a little butter or oil in the bottom of a deep pan, place it over a low heat and stir the chopped up vegetables round with a wooden spoon and let them literally sweat it out in their own juices until they just reach the crunchy stage.

The ordinary boiled potato responds to gentler treatment than most people give it. Try doing it this way and notice the difference! Barely cover the potatoes with water, put a tight lid on your pan - a round of foil between pan and lid is better still - bring them up to the boil and let them gently simmer until they are cooked, not mushy.

New potatoes are perfection if put into boiling water and gently simmered till cooked. Swished round in the pan afterwards with a knob of butter, and sprinkled with chopped mint, they are gorgeous enough to be a meal in themselves.

New potatoes too make a delicious potato salad and here's a tip: put your salad dressing on when the potatoes are still hot; this way it soaks right into the potatoes, and the result is less oily and far more flavoursome than putting it on when they are cold. A potato salad is also improved by making it the day before and letting the potatoes marinade, as it were, in the dressing.

By the way, save the water from cooking potatoes and vegetables for making stocks and sauces - its full of all the valuable mineral salts and vitamins. Though remember, stock made with leaf vegetables won't keep well, so add it only to soup which is going to be all eaten at once.

Some of the recipes using vegetables to look out for in my collection: Colonial Stew made with carrots, turnips, onions, cabbage, beetroot; Lamb and Cabbage Hotpot; Sauté Spring Potatoes (made with new potatoes and spring onions); Chicken Pot Roast with a medley of vegetables; Country Vegetarian Pie; Leek, Egg and Potato Nests; Potato Cauliflower au Gratin; Mixed Vegetable Curry; Cauliflower and Bacon Crisp; Spinach Pie.

Notice the big bunch of parsley in the left hand side of the picture. If you have a garden or even a window box, try to grow a clump of it. Apart from its pretty look sprinkled over sauces and vegetables, it's full of Vitamin C.

Summer meals are missing a dimension without a green salad, but when your garden lettuce has bolted and the shop ones are at silly prices, try a salad of shredded cabbage. I make my own version: very finely shredded heart of crisp cabbage, thin circlets of leek or spring onion, raisins (plumped out first in hot water), and for colour and extra taste, chopped radish sprinkled on top.

5

I love talking about soup. To me it's almost the most important part of a meal, or, as so many families today are discovering, a lovely big bowl of home-made soup can be a meal in itself, containing all the nourishment any growing family could wish for. Easier too, on a housewife's time, for large quantities of soup can be made ahead.

All these three soups in the picture are based on stock, and for those of you who have not got into the habit of making stock or have never tried it because it sounds too complicated, let me tell you it's the easiest thing in the world. If you are an inveterate hoarder of things like I am, you'll be an excellent stock maker, for it's very satisfying to make something of value from what most people would throw away, or which cost mere pence from your butcher. Stock cubes are convenient when you're in a hurry, but only a substitute for the real thing, as old hands at stock-making already know.

There are basically two kinds of stock; one is made from poultry bones and the other from meat bones (there's a third if you count game bones, but these aren't always available to the town based housewife). The first is used for white soups like Chicken, Celery, Potato, Leek, etc., and those soups for which you wish to retain the colour of the main ingredient. The second is for brown soups - those with a meaty taste.

The directions for making stock are simple. Put the carcass and any odd bits of attached flesh, gristle or skin into a pan, cover with water, bring slowly to the boil. Skim off the froth. Boil for a few minutes, then reduce heat until the water is just trembling and leave it for a couple of hours on a low heat on the hob or inside the oven until the bones are soft and fall apart. Strain then leave to cool. When absolutely cold, you'll find it has become a rich jelly which can be stored in the fridge or cold larder. By the way, if you are storing meat stock for more than a few days give it a reboil to keep it fresh. Stock always freezes well. Put it in ½ to 1 pint containers so that you take out small amounts at a time for making soups and stews.

In the tureen at the top of the picture is *Suppertime Soup* which contains chopped bacon and onion fried together and added to diced new potatoes that have been cooked in chicken stock. Noodles - from the Italian countryside - contribute a change of scene. They are very nourishing and look pretty floating in a soup. They can be bought at most grocers and supermarkets. The soup in the middle - *Potato Peasant Soup,* is a real wintertime soup. It's one I call my package-deal soup for those having to rush in for a quick meal and out again. They don't even have to bother with the bread and cheese part of the meal - it's all in the soup.

The rich-looking tureenful of soup at the bottom of the picture is called *Celestial Soup* and is based on beef stock (bones or a cube) with onions and potatoes, and a spot of sherry for a really Heavenly flavour.

In my youth, fish was no stranger on our menu. Scotland is a great place for fish - the rivers are full of trout and salmon and from the many ports come sea-fish of all sorts into our towns and cities - always beautifully fresh. Trout came into our house from time to time from neighbours with sons who spent their holidays with rod and line down at the little burns.

With the exception of fish and chips, we are not over-enthusiastic fish eaters in this country. I often wonder if it's because we mostly eat it overcooked. For, unlike meat, which can be enjoyed all the way from rare to well-done, fish, given one extra minute past the just-cooked stage, becomes coarse and tasteless. One good reason we like our fish from the chip shop is that inside its protective coating of batter the fish remains moist and succulent. My rule is when in doubt, undercook fish because, containing so much moisture, it is cooking away in its own juice before even the butter or oil in the pan gets going.

Here are three rules for cooking fish: Firstly, when frying in shallow fat, don't let it cook beyond a tiny frizzle. Secondly, with deep-fat frying the fish will be perfectly cooked when the batter or crumbs turn pale gold. Thirdly, when poaching or boiling fish in water, wrap it in foil, don't let the water boil fiercely and allow the fish to cool in the liquor to retain its moisture.

The trout recipe I give you is one of those glamorous recipes I told you I had included. For trout, unless you have a fisherman in the family or have fishing friends who bring you gifts, is very expensive. On the other hand, a little of it goes a long way, for like salmon it is one of the meatiest of fish. My recipe for Stuffed Trout with Lemon Sauce makes it go even further for the stuffing is composed of Potato and Mushrooms mixed with cream (the ingredients on the plate alongside the fish). We used to serve it in the little Inverness hotel my husband and I once owned, for people who booked a table for a special occasion.

Dogger Bank Pie is at the other end of the budget spectrum for its main ingredient is cod, which is still quite reasonably priced. Again, a full-bodied fish, which does not shrink with cooking, and with the added potatoes, leeks and mushrooms, makes a delicious and economic dish.

I am particularly attached to the next recipe in the picture - Poacher's Tasties - because they are so versatile. They would be right for any meal - even breakfast. For a main meal, serve them with vegetables, cold with a salad, or alone as a starter to a dinner party. Take them wrapped in foil to a picnic or made half the size stated in the recipe; they make a marvellous cocktail snack. These pasties can, of course, be made with real salmon which puts them in a class of their own, but between you and me I actually find them tastier made with the canned salmon.

Pictures, like tunes, are very evocative of past events and this one of a magnificent Roast Rib of Beef takes me back to Sundays on our farm when my Father would take me with him to Edinburgh to deliver the milk from our dairy herd. We'd leave at 6.00 in the morning, and be back in time to walk two miles to Church. It was a long day for a small girl of seven, but an eventful one in our quiet lives, and I have to admit the highlight of it was Sunday lunch. Many a sermon I've sat through with my mouth watering thinking of that succulent roast awaiting me.

Even in those days a large joint of beef was a treat, but nowadays it's a positive luxury at the price it is. On the other hand, in terms of pound weight of meat, a rib roast is, in fact, an economic joint because there's not a bit of it wasted.

Like love and marriage, potatoes and roast beef are inseparable. Traditionally they are roast potatoes, for which I give you a recipe

9

further on, but there are several other ways to cook them, all of which go well with a roast joint.

In this picture surrounding the beef you will find potatoes cooked seven different ways. Starting on the left at the back you will see Pommes Duchesse which I find very popular with people today because apart from looking a bit special they freeze well, unlike most cooked potatoes, which means the housewife can cook a large batch at one time. Next come those traditional roast potatoes - called Boston Roast Potatoes, named after the famous old town in Lincolnshire - the largest potato growing area in England. You might not think it necessary to give a recipe for plain roast potatoes, but people are always asking me the secret of getting roast potatoes really crunchy crisp and this recipe tells you exactly how. Below are Potato Rings which are dipped in egg, sage and onion, and fried till cooked - unusual, and the herby taste is a good foil to the beef. In front are Golden Leaves for which peeled potatoes are grated - yes grated - perhaps you have never tried this, but it is very easily done and the result is well worth the little extra time. The grated potatoes are mixed with seasoning and beaten eggs, spoonfuls of which are fried in fat until golden brown. They should be flattened in the pan to leaf thickness - hence the name. Behind these are Pommes Dauphine which are made from traditional ingredients with rather exotic overtones. They have now been cooked in British kitchens for many years, and I like to think that a British chef went over to the French court, and appreciating the French taste for fancy dishes, dressed up our plain breadcrumbed potatoes in a choux pastry jacket and dedicated them to the Dauphin. Behind these in the picture you will see Sauté Spring Potatoes, which are new potatoes fried in a mixture of chopped spring onions and dry mustard until golden. Lastly, Batter Potatoes which could be made from left-over boiled potatoes. They are simply sliced, dipped into batter, chopped mixed herbs, and fried in deep fat.

Armed with a knife, fork and spoon, I almost feel I could dump myself down among the poppies and daisies in this next picture and start right in eating. Particularly the Meat Loaf on the blue and white plate, which has been a special favourite of mine and my family for many years. It's made with equal quantities of best beef mince, sausage meat and minced bacon, with grated potatoes and spice. You steam it in a pudding basin for a couple of hours and then eat it hot with vegetables or cold with salad. For a touch of glamour, serve it with a sweet-sour sauce made with chutney, mayonnaise and mustard mixed well together. This freezes well, so why not, when you're making one for a current meal, do another for the freezer; it takes no longer to make two than one. You can use a pudding basin or a foil one which you can buy from any freezer supplier.

The rather colourful round dish in the front of the picture contains a recipe called Madelein's Pork Pie. Bit of a mystery dish, as I'm sure you won't have guessed the ingredients. The main ingredient is pig's liver and sausage meat, topped with whipped potato mixed with an equal quantity of grated carrot. A good dish for children who are not always keen on carrot; but disguised in this way I find they gobble it up.

Right at the back of the photograph is a dish called Beef Soufflé - not in fact a soufflé, but so called because the potato topping, to what is a

classic Shepherd's Pie mixture is whipped up with stiffened whites of egg.

There's a veal dish in front. Seville Veal with Crispy Fries - one of my special occasion dishes, but quick and easy. Veal fillets are fried gently and served with a sauce made with orange slices simmered in butter and orange juice. The potatoes alongside them go particularly well with this recipe but could be cooked in this way for many other dishes as well. I call them Crispy Fries and they are an original alternative to chips. The potatoes are grated and mixed with pepper and salt and a little thyme, placed in spoonfuls in the pan and cooked in butter till crisp.

Poultry and game are usually frequent items on a farm family menu. When my Mother's hens had done their stint of egg laying, she used to cook them for us as Chicken Pot Roast for after a long career of laying they were far too tough for anything but slow cooking. But cooked this way, long and slow in a heavy pan with a medley of vegetables and small new potatoes, they are absolutely delicious and provide a complete meal in one pan. Think of the washing-up you save! Boiling-fowls which all poulterers and supermarkets provide the year round are far cheaper than roasters, and have, I think, a lot more flavour. The carcass makes a super stock.

As for game, there were always plenty of hares and pigeons brought into our kitchen, especially around February when my Father would take his gun out and clobber them feeding on his young corn. Some poulterers have both for sale and they are about the cheapest meat on the market.

There are countless recipes for hare, but I find plain Casserole of Hare with Potato Dumplings the tastiest way and what beautiful rich gravy you get with it. The dumplings which you can see in the Hare Casserole, are made with potatoes - one of the best ways of using up left-over potatoes. You cook them in boiling water and add them to the casserole at the last minute.

After the meat is finished, you can add a bit of vegetable stock to what's left of the gravy for one of the best-ever soups. Serve it with a big bowl of freshly boiled floury potatoes to dunk in the soup. Another meal in itself.

There are just as many recipes for wood pigeon, all coming from country kitchens. In the old days it was sometimes the only sort of meat a cottager would get, and the country wife had to learn to be inventive to relieve the monotony. But don't think because of that pigeons are dull meat - anything but. Cooked properly, they can be as delicious as any game. I have favourite ways of cooking them. One - if I know it to be a young bird, I roast it like any other game bird, that is to say I lay strips of fat bacon over the breast and pour a little butter or oil over it and roast it in the oven at 400°F. or Gas Mark 6, for about ten minutes, basting frequently as there is little natural fat in a pigeon. The second way is a lazy way, and this applies to any age of bird, but the result is delicious. I cut out the breasts only and throw the rest away. Then I skin these, flatten them with a rolling pin, and cook them as for Veal Escallops (i.e. dipped in egg and breadcrumbs and fried in butter). The third way is to casserole them. Follow the hare casserole recipe and you can't go wrong. This recipe is particularly good when you are not sure of the bird's age.

There's nothing so tough as an old pigeon so it needs long slow cooking. Don't forget that the carcass can be boiled up to make good brown stock.

Born and raised a real down-to-earth Scots girl, baking is my favourite kind of cooking. If I may be a bit immodest, the Scotswoman is known the world over for her baking and I was brought up in the tradition. When my Mother made Drop Scones, it was my job as a small girl to stand beside her at the stove and flip them over when they were cooked on one side. We had plenty of practice with baking, my sisters and I, for we always had friends and neighbours dropping in for tea. Sometimes on a Sunday we would sit down twenty-five at the table.

Spread out on this cloth in the picture which, incidentally, I embroidered myself many years ago, is some of the tea-time fare my Mother used to make regularly. Every farmhouse had its weekly bake in those days and if I close my eyes even now, I can still conjure up the delicious smells which came from our kitchen. We children had to watch our step when our Mother was baking, and Father used to find any excuse to be away from the house. But the result was well worth our caution and tact. Traditional Potato Scones were, and still are, my favourite - those are the ones in the picture with the little toast marks on them. They are easy to make and if you have a freezer do a double batch to put away for next time. Pop them into the oven to warm before the meal and the butter will sink into them.

Potato Oatcakes are much easier to make than ordinary oat cakes as they are more substantial and don't break so easily. In the picture, you can see them to the right of the Potato Scones. They are delicious for tea with butter and honey or for lunch or supper with soup or cheese.

I am giving you this recipe for Potato Wholemeal Bread because it is not only a good way to use up left-over potato, but it will come in handy if and when we get any more of those strikes when flour is short and bread non-existent. If, up to now, you have fought a bit shy of making your own bread because it has seemed an added undertaking in your busy life, do try it. My recipe is a simple one and once the family has tasted it, you'll never be allowed to bring another bought loaf into the house! I find home-made bread very bribable stuff! 'Sorry, no more until someone helps me peel the spuds!'

The children will love these Doughnuts and they're much easier and quicker than the sort you make with yeast. Put a plate of them on the tea-table for the children on their return from school and see if you have any left! Almond tart, at the top - made with potato - is my version of the traditional Bakewell Tart. It was first made in the little town of Bakewell, Derbyshire, a hundred years ago, and is still a favourite with everyone.

Potato and Prawn Soup

Celestial Soup

Highland Soup

serves 4

2 lb [1 kg] **potatoes**
½ **cucumber**
1 leek
1½ pints [750 ml] **white stock**
2-3 tablespoons [2-3 × 20 ml spoons] **cream**
squeeze of lemon juice
3-4 oz [75-100 g] **prawns**
3 fl oz [75 ml] **white wine**
1 oz [25 g] **butter**
salt and pepper
2 oz [50 g] **chives, chopped**

Melt the butter in a pan and add to it the thinly sliced leek and peeled diced cucumber.
Sweat without browning, and add the potatoes, then cook for another few minutes.
Add 1½ pints (750 ml) stock and seasoning and a little chopped chive.
Cook for approx. 40 minutes until all the ingredients are tender.
Liquidize soup to a fine purée and add the single cream, wine, lemon juice and prawns.
Correct the seasoning.
Mix together and then leave the soup to cool.
Serve with chopped chives sprinkled on top.

serves 4

1 lb [500 g] **potatoes**
12 oz [375 g] **carrots**
2 onions of medium size
2 oz [50 g] **butter**
2 pints [1 l] **beef stock**
a pinch of nutmeg
a little sugar (optional)
sherry and cream to flavour
salt and pepper
parsley, chopped

Peel the potatoes thinly and cut into quarters.
Scrape the carrots and cut into pieces.
Peel and slice the onions.
Melt the butter in a pan and add all the vegetables.
Shake pan over heat for a minute.
Add stock, salt and pepper.
Simmer until vegetables are soft.
Rub through a sieve or liquidise and return to pan.
Add a pinch of nutmeg, sherry to flavour and cream.
Reheat and serve with chopped parsley or fried croûtons.

serves 4

6 large potatoes
6 leeks
2 oz [50 g] **butter**
3 pints [1½ l] **white stock**
chives, chopped
salt
black pepper

Cut the vegetables into pieces.
Fry in the butter till golden.
Add the stock and salt, and simmer for 1½ hours.
Sieve or liquidise.
Return to the pan.
Add the chives and black pepper.
Return to boil for about 4-5 minutes.

Here's tae us-
Wha's like us?

18

Brussels Sprouts and Potato Soup

Potato and Avocado Pear Soup

Parsley (Petroselinum Crispum)

If your system lacks Vitamin A, think before wasting parsley as a garnish or a seasoning for soup, or not eating it at all. It is one of the richest food sources of vitamins and minerals. In comparison to the Vitamin A content of carrots (5500 units) parsley offers at least 40,000 units per ounce, which also is about four times that of spinach. Moreover it contains as much Vitamin C as orange, and an appreciable quantity of Vitamin B factors, thiamin, riboflavin and niacin.

Parsley contains these four vital minerals: calcium, copper, iron and manganese — the better to strengthen and 'purify' your bloodstream.

Both parsley leaves and seeds (ripe fruits) possess medicinal virtues.

Eat a handful of parsley to mask the tale-telling odours of liquors, onions and garlic.

Ben Charles Harris
A Culinary Herbal

serves 4

8 oz [250 g] potatoes
8 oz [250 g] brussels sprouts
1 onion
1 pint [500 ml] water
¼ pint [125 ml] milk
salt and pepper

Prepare the sprouts, toss into boiling water and strain after 2 minutes.
Peel and cut up potatoes and onion, place in a pan with the water and seasoning and bring to the boil.
Add the sprouts and simmer gently for 20-25 minutes.
Pass through a sieve or liquidise. Add milk and colouring if needed. Adjust seasoning.
Reheat before serving.

Potato Vegetable Soup

serves 4

4-5 medium sized potatoes, diced
1 leek, finely chopped
1 onion, finely chopped
1 carrot, finely grated
parsley, chopped
2 pints [1 l] stock
salt and pepper
1 oz [25 g] butter

Melt the butter in a pan; add the potatoes, leek and onion, and sauté over a gentle heat.
Add the stock and seasoning and simmer gently until the vegetables are soft.
When serving, garnish with carrot and parsley.

serves 4

8 oz [250 g] potatoes, peeled and diced
1 onion, peeled and chopped
1 clove garlic, crushed
2 oz [50 g] butter
2 ripe Avocado pears, peeled and de-stoned
1 teaspoon [1×5 ml spoon] curry powder
1 pint [500 ml] stock
2 teaspoons [2×5 ml spoons] lemon juice
salt and pepper
Croûtons:
cubes of bread
fat for frying

Prepare the vegetables.
Lightly fry the onion, garlic and potatoes in the melted butter.
Add the chopped avocado pears to the pan with a little of the curry powder.
Cover with stock, bring to the boil and then simmer for 20 minutes.
Pass through a sieve or liquidise.
Reheat, and season to taste. Add the lemon juice.
Serve garnished with croûtons of fried bread.

Cottage Soup

serves 4

3 large potatoes
1 teacup smoked bacon, small
   dice
½ oz [12.5 g] butter
1 small turnip
1 medium onion
1 carrot
2 pints [1 l] stock
Cheddar cheese, grated
salt and pepper

Melt the fat in a pan, add the
bacon and cook till brown.
Add the grated potatoes, turnip,
onion, and carrot with stock.
Season.
Season with salt and pepper.
Boil gently till the vegetables and
meat are tender - about ¾ hour.
Serve piping hot, garnished with
grated cheese.

Cold Soup

serves 4

white part of six leeks, cut in
   cubes
10 oz [300 g] potatoes
1½ oz [35 g] butter
nutmeg
clove of garlic
1 pint [500 ml] chicken stock
½ pint [250 ml] single cream
salt and pepper

Sauté the leeks in butter and add
the potatoes, salt, pepper and
nutmeg.
Add the stock and simmer for
25 minutes.
Pass through a sieve or liquidise.
Add the clove of garlic. Chill.
Before serving, remove the garlic
and stir in the cream.

Potato and
Green Pea Soup

serves 4

8 oz [250 g] potatoes
12 oz [375 g] peas, shelled
2 small onions
½ oz [12.5 g] butter
½ teaspoon [2.5 ml] sugar
a sprig of mint
1 pint [500 ml] water
salt and pepper

Peel and quarter the potatoes and
onions.
Bring the water to the boil and
add the vegetables, mint, salt,
pepper and sugar.
Simmer for 30 minutes.
Pass through a sieve or liquidise
and adjust seasoning.
Stir in the butter while reheating
the soup.

Potato Peasant
Soup

serves 4

1 lb [500 g] potatoes
1 onion
1 leek
1 oz [25 g] butter
1 pint [500 ml] stock or water
½ pint [250 ml] milk
2 slices crusty bread, cut into dice
2 oz [50 g] Cheddar cheese, grated
salt and pepper

Peel and cut up the potatoes.
Dice the onion and leek and toss
in the melted butter.
Add the stock, potatoes and
seasoning and simmer until the
vegetables are tender.
Sieve the soup and return to the
pan, then stir in the milk and
season to taste.
Place the bread in a tureen and
pour over the hot soup.
Sprinkle with the cheese.

Suppertime Soup

serves 4

1 lb [500 g] **new potatoes**
2 pints [1 l] **chicken stock**
4 oz [100 g] **noodles**
4 oz [100 g] **bacon**
1 **large onion**
Parmesan cheese
salt and pepper

Scrape the potatoes and cut into small dice.
Cook the potatoes in stock until tender.
Cook the noodles until soft and add to the potatoes.
Cut the bacon into small pieces and fry with the finely chopped onion.
Stir into the soup and season.
Serve piping hot, sprinkled with Parmesan cheese.

Chestnut Potato Soup

serves 6-8

1 lb [500 g] **potatoes, peeled and sliced**
1 can **chestnut purée**
2 leeks, **washed and chopped**
1 bunch **watercress**
1 oz [25 g] **butter**
1¼ pints [625 ml] **stock**
1¼ pints [625 ml] **cream or milk**
salt and pepper

Prepare the vegetables, melt the butter and fry the potatoes and leeks for 2-3 minutes. Season.
Stir in the chestnut purée, and add the cress and stock.
Simmer for 30-40 minutes; then sieve or liquidize.
Re-season, and before serving add the cream or milk, being careful not to boil.

Potato and Watercress Soup

serves 4

1 lb [500 g] **potatoes, peeled and thinly sliced**
½ large **onion, chopped**
1 bunch **watercress, chopped**
1 pint [500 ml] **stock**
¼ pint [125 ml] **milk**
a little **grated nutmeg**
salt and pepper

Place potatoes, onions, half the watercress and stock in a pan. Season.
Bring to the boil and allow to cook.
Sieve or liquidize; return to the heat and add the milk.
Reheat and adjust seasoning.
Garnish with the remainder of the chopped watercress.

A Centipede was happy quite
   Until a Toad in fun
Said, 'Pray, which leg moves after which?'
   This raised her doubts to such a pitch
She fell exhausted in the ditch,
   Not knowing how to run.

Travellers' Pie

Hamburgers in Wine Sauce

serves 4

Potato Pastry:
4 oz [100 g] potatoes, sieved or riced
5 oz [125 g] plain flour
3 oz [75 g] butter
1 teaspoon [1×5 ml spoon] baking powder
a pinch of salt
Filling:
6 oz [150 g] mild Cheddar cheese, grated
4 eggs
1 tablespoon [1 x 20 ml spoon] parsley, chopped
salt and pepper

Make the pastry by creaming the butter till soft. Add the potatoes, flour, baking powder and salt and blend well together.
Turn out onto a floured board and knead very lightly.
Divide into two and roll out to about ¼ inch (0.5 cm) thick. Place on a greased ovenproof plate and prick with a fork.
Sprinkle the cheese over the pastry, making four hollows, and break the eggs into these hollows.
Season with salt and pepper and sprinkle with the parsley.
Roll out the remaining pastry to cover, knock up the edges, and flute with the fingers.
Brush over with milk and make a slit in the centre of the pastry.
Place in the oven and bake at 400°F (200°C), Gas Mark 6, for 35 minutes.
Serve with green salad.

Pot-Pourri

Pot-pourri is derived from the French and means to rot. It describes the old art of preserving the precious floral scents of herbs by placing their dried petals or flower heads in jars, with salt added. 'This custom' wrote Lillian M. Cronk in Home Garden, 'originated in ancient times when people needed sweet romantic scents to relieve the oppressive air that accumulated in their damp, poorly ventilated and almost windowless dwelling houses.'

Ben Charles Harris

serves 4

8 oz [250 g] potato, cooked and sieved
8 oz [250 g] raw minced beef
8 oz [250 g] raw minced pork
1 egg
grated rind of ½ a lemon
a pinch of nutmeg
2 oz [50 g] melted butter
2 slices stale bread softened in water and pressed dry
salt and pepper

Mix all the ingredients together, seasoning well, and divide into 8 portions.

Sauce:
2 oz [50 g] butter or margarine
1 tablespoon [1×20 ml spoon] parsley, chopped
1 tablespoon [1×20 ml spoon] chives or shallots, chopped
juice of ½ a lemon
½ cup dry white or red wine

Melt the butter in a frying pan, add the parsley and chives and sauté for 5 minutes.
Add the hamburgers and brown them quickly on both sides.
Lower the heat and add the lemon juice and wine.
Cover the pan and cook gently for 15 minutes.

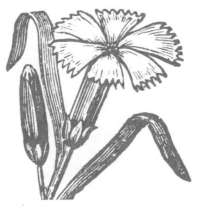

Potato and Cheese Custard

serves 4

1 lb [500 g] **potatoes, peeled, boiled and sliced**
4 oz [100 g] **Cheddar cheese, grated**
4 oz [100 g] **bacon, cooked and diced**
2 **eggs**
½ pint [250 ml] **milk**
salt and pepper

Grease an ovenproof dish, then place alternate layers of potatoes, cheese and bacon in it, ending with cheese.
Beat the eggs, add the milk and seasoning and pour over the potatoes.
Bake in a slow oven, 350°F (180°C), Gas Mark 4, for 40-45 minutes.

Potato Meat Mould

serves 4

8 oz [250 g] **potatoes, peeled**
8 oz [250 g] **steak mince**
8 oz [250 g] **bacon, minced**
8 oz [250 g] **pork sausage meat**
2 **eggs**
1 **onion, finely chopped or grated**
nutmeg
pepper

Grate the potato into a bowl and pour off the excess water.
Add the steak mince, minced bacon, sausage meat, egg, onion, pepper and nutmeg.
Mix well together until the ingredients are thoroughly blended, and transfer to a greased 1 pint (500 ml) pudding basin.
Cover with foil.
Place in a pan of boiling water and simmer for 2½ hours, topping up with water when necessary.
Allow to cool in the bowl, loosen from the sides with a knife and turn on to a serving dish.
Serve with a mixed salad.
Note:
This can also be eaten hot and served with an onion sauce.

Bacon Pancake

serves 4

1 **large potato**
4 oz [100 g] **bacon rashers**
1 **small onion**
1 **egg**
1 oz [25 g] **flour**
Worcestershire sauce
oil
salt and pepper

Remove the rinds from the bacon and chop into small pieces.
Grate the potato and onion coarsely.
Mix all the ingredients together.
Heat a little oil in a frying pan, pour in the mixture, and cook for 7 minutes on each side.

Peanut and Potato Scotch Egg

serves 4

8 oz [250 g] **potatoes, mashed**
1 **egg, slightly beaten**
4 **hard boiled eggs**
salted peanuts, finely chopped
salt and pepper
fat for frying

Beat together the mashed potato and half the raw egg with salt and pepper.
Surround each hard-boiled egg with the potato.
Coat with the remainder of the raw egg and roll in chopped peanuts.
Fry in deep fat until golden brown.
Drain on kitchen paper and serve hot or cold with salad.

Potato Omelette

Savoury Potatojacks

Potato Pâté Balls

serves 4

1 lb [500 g] **potatoes, sieved or riced**
3 eggs, separated
parsley
1 oz [25 g] **butter**
salt and pepper

Add the egg yolks to the potatoes, salt and pepper and beat well together.
Whisk the whites till stiff and fold gently into the potatoes.
Melt a little butter in an omelette pan, add the mixture and brown.
Turn, and brown the other side.
Turn out onto a serving plate and garnish with chopped parsley. For variation, any cooked meats or fish can be added.

serves 4

1½ lb [750 g] **potatoes, boiled**
1 egg
1 onion, peeled and chopped
2 oz [50 g] **Cheddar cheese, grated**
2 oz [50 g] **bacon, rind removed diced and cooked**
an egg for each round
salt and pepper

Mix together all the ingredients, binding together with the egg, and season to taste.
Form into rounds, using a little flour.
Fry lightly in a greased pan until golden brown.
Serve topped with a fried or poached egg.

serves 4

1½ lb [750 g] **potatoes, mashed**
1 oz [25 g] **butter**
1 egg, beaten
13½ oz can of pâté
browned breadcrumbs (or chopped salted peanuts)
a second beaten egg
oil
salt and pepper

Beat the melted butter into the potatoes and add the lightly beaten egg. Season to taste.
Roll the pâté into 8 small balls; surround each with mashed potato and mould into ball shapes.
Dip the balls into beaten egg and coat with breadcrumbs or chopped salted nuts.
Fry in deep fat until golden brown.

It has been said that the hedgehog interrupts his winter sleep on February 2nd, and emerges to take stock of the weather. Paradoxically, if the sun is shining and he sees his own shadow, he goes back for another six weeks of hibernation, while if it is dull and no shadow is cast, spring is just around the corner.

24

Corned Beef and Potato Flan

serves 4

4 oz [100 g] **potato, cooked and diced**
4 oz [100 g] **corned beef**
2 oz [50 g] **cooked peas**
½ oz [12.5 g] **butter**
½ oz [12.5 g] **flour**
4 tablespoons [4×20 ml spoons] **milk**
1 **beaten egg**
1 oz [25 g] **cheese, grated**
6 oz [150 g] **shortcrust pastry**
salt and pepper

Roll out the pastry to line a 7 inch (18 cm) flan ring.
Chop the corned beef and combine with the potatoes and peas.
Melt the butter in a pan. Add the flour and allow to cook without browning.
Add the milk gradually and cook till it boils and thickens.
Stir in the beef, potatoes and peas.
Add the beaten egg, cheese and seasoning and spoon into the flan case.
Bake for 10 minutes at 425°F (220°C), Gas Mark 7.
Reduce the heat to 375°F (190°C), Gas Mark 5, and bake for 12-15 minutes.
Can be served hot or cold.

Cheese and Potato Sticks

serves 4

4 oz [100 g] **potatoes, sieved or riced**
4 oz [100 g] **plain flour**
pinch mustard
pinch nutmeg
4 oz [100 g] **butter**
4 oz [100 g] **Cheddar cheese, grated**
1 **egg, beaten**
salt and pepper

Mix together the potato, flour, mustard, nutmeg and salt and pepper.
Rub in the butter to make a soft dough.
Add the cheese and lay aside to chill for one hour in a refrigerator.
Roll out thinly and brush with beaten egg.
Cut into sticks 4 inches (10 cm) long by ¼ inch (0.5 cm) wide and place on a greased baking sheet, then bake in a moderate oven 350°F (180°C) Gas Mark 4 until brown. Store in an airtight tin.

Liver Meat Loaf

serves 4

8 oz [250 g] **potatoes, sieved or riced**
1 lb [500 g] **liver**
1 lb [500 g] **pork sausage meat**
2 oz [50 g] **butter or oil**
2 oz [50 g] **onion, finely chopped**
2 oz [50 g] **celery, finely chopped**
1 **egg, beaten**
¼ pint [125 ml] **tomato juice**
salt and pepper

Brown the liver in hot fat, then remove from the pan and mince.
Add the celery and onion to the fat and cook for 2-3 minutes.
Mix all the ingredients together using sufficient tomato juice to make a moist texture.
Press into a greased loaf tin and bake at 350°F (180°C), Gas Mark 4, for 1½-2 hours.
Serve hot with onion sauce, or cold with salad.

Potato Bridies

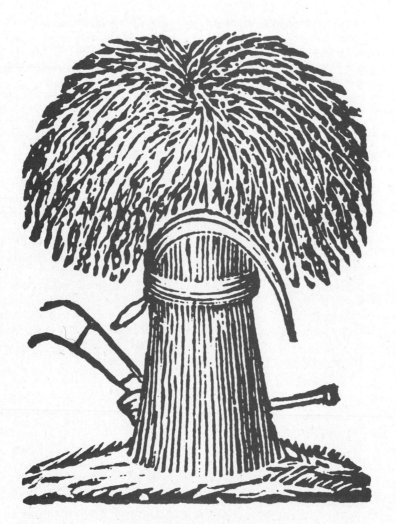

Maybe this first crept into the Christian calendar as a remnant of a pagan ritual, but many farmers still take their ploughs to church to be blessed to bring home good harvests.

serves 4

1 lb [500 g] **Duchesse potato mixture (see recipe page 109)**
4 oz [100 g] **minced beef, cooked**
approx 2 tablespoons [2×20 ml spoons] **thick brown gravy or tomato sauce**
egg and breadcrumbs
parsley, chopped

Mix together the minced beef and enough gravy to bind.
Divide the potato into small portions and place some of the meat mixture on each one.
Using a little flour to help, seal the edges so that the meat is hidden inside the potato.
Flatten the bridies and coat with egg and breadcrumbs.
Fry in deep fat until golden brown.
Drain on absorbent paper and serve sprinkled with chopped parsley.

Egg Fritters

serves 4

1 lb [500 g] **potatoes, peeled**
2 eggs + 4 poached eggs
oil
salt and pepper
parsley, chopped

Grate the raw potatoes.
Beat the eggs with salt and pepper and mix with the potatoes.
Fry in large tablespoonfuls, (20 ml spoon) flattened out, allowing approx. 5 minutes to each side. Drain.
Place a poached egg on each circle and garnish with parsley.

Wigtown Potatoes

serves 4

1½ lb [750 g] **tiny new potatoes, scraped**
1½ oz [35 g] **butter**
6 oz [150 g] **mushrooms, sliced**
1 tablespoon [1×20 ml spoon] **thyme, chopped**
1 tablespoon [1×20 ml spoon] **chives, chopped**
juice of one lemon
salt and pepper

Melt the butter in a heavy based pan, add the potatoes, and coat with the butter.
Add the mushrooms and herbs, season.
Put buttered paper over the vegetables, cover with the saucepan lid and cook gently over a low heat, shaking the pan occasionally, for 30 minutes.
Remove the lid and paper, pour in the lemon juice and bring to the boil.
Serve immediately.

Bromsgrove

serves 4

8 oz [250 g] **potatoes, cooked**
4 oz [100 g] **ham**
1 tablespoon [1×20 ml spoon] **parsley, chopped**
Worcestershire sauce
a little mustard
2 eggs
½ pint [250 ml] **milk**
salt and pepper

Beat together the eggs, milk, parsley, sauce, mustard, salt and pepper.
Chop the potatoes and ham finely, and place in a buttered loaf tin.
Pour over the egg mixture, and bake in a tin of water for 1½ hours in a slow oven 300°F (150°C), Gas Mark 2.
Turn out of the tin when cold.

Stuffed Potatoes

serves 4

4 large potatoes
Stuffing:
½ lb [250 g] **cooked minced meat**
1 teaspoon [1×5 ml spoon] **parsley, chopped**
2 oz [50 g] **butter**
1 onion, finely chopped
½ pint [250 ml] **well seasoned stock**
salt and pepper

Peel the potatoes and slice the top from each one.
Scoop out the inside and fill with the stuffing.
Replace the lids and place the potatoes in hot fat in a baking dish.
Cover the dish and bake at 400°F (200°C), Gas Mark 6, for one hour.
Baste the potatoes occasionally during cooking.
(Boil the scooped out potato and use in another dish).

Cheese, Tomato and Potato Flan

serves 4

1 lb [500 g] **potatoes, sieved or rices**
1 teaspoon [1×5 ml spoon] **mixed herbs**
1 teaspoon [1×5 ml spoon] **Parmesan cheese**
1 **egg yolk**
1 **large onion, chopped**
2 tablespoons [2×20 ml spoons] **oil**
8 oz can **tomatoes**
4 oz [100 g] **Cheddar cheese, grated**
2 **stuffed olives, thinly sliced**
1 **small can anchovy fillets**
salt and pepper

Add the herbs, Parmesan cheese and egg yolk to the potatoes and beat till smooth.
Press the mixture on to the base and up the sides of a large, greased ovenproof plate.
Place in the oven and bake at 400°F (200°C), Gas Mark 6 for 20 minutes.
Fry the onion in oil and drain well.
Cover the potato with layers of onion, tomato and cheese.
Cook for 20 minutes at 400°F (200°C), Gas Mark 6.
Garnish with anchovy fillets and sliced stuffed olives.

Cheese and Egg Pie

serves 4

1 lb [500 g] **potatoes, peeled**
4 **eggs, hard boiled**
¾ pint [375 ml] **white sauce**
4 oz [100 g] **Cheddar cheese, grated**
salt and pepper

Slice the potatoes thickly, and then parboil for 5 minutes.
Grease the bottom of an ovenproof dish and sprinkle with half the cheese.
Slice the eggs, then arrange alternate layers of sliced potatoes and eggs, starting with potatoes.
Cover with the sauce, then sprinkle with grated cheese.
Cook until the top is browned, 375°F (190°C), Gas Mark 5, for approx. 35 minutes.

A Herb Pillow for Sleep

Herb pillows are just bags stuffed with herbs. Quite apart from their use to induce sleep, herb pillows are refreshing and pleasant to anyone who is ill, or recovering from an illness, and perhaps in hospital where the pervading smell is of antiseptics and anaesthetics; for elderly or anyone who is wholly or partially bed-ridden. A nice small herb pillow makes a wonderful present for a sick friend, far better than a bunch of grapes (which the nurses will eat) or a box of chocolates (which everyone will eat), or even a bunch of flowers which will die too soon in a stuffy bedroom or hospital ward.

A few bruised fresh marjoram leaves, put inside a pillow case, will induce sleep, but smell far too strongly to fill a whole pillow.

Dried hops are most commonly used in pillows to induce sleep. Garden Mignonette has the same effect, and can be included in pillow mixtures, such as the following:
Equal parts of: peppermint, sage, lemon balm, half as much again of lavender.

Then add the following to total half as much again as all of these: dill, marjoram, thyme, tarragon, angelica, Sweet Cecily, rosemary, red bergamot, lemon verbena and lemon thyme.

But do vary the herbs or leave out any you don't like, and be sure the herbs are dry before use, or mustiness will pervade the lot.

Suzanne Beedell

Timbale of Potatoes

serves 4

2 lb [1 kg] **potatoes, sieved**
2 egg yolks
pinch grated nutmeg
1 oz [25 g] **butter**
1 lb [500 g] **cooked mixed vegetables**
4 hard boiled eggs, chopped
¼ pint [125 ml] **cheese sauce**
salt and pepper

Put the potato, butter and egg yolks in a pan and beat together.
Season to taste.
Pipe the potato into a decorative border 2 inch (5 cm) high onto an ovenproof plate, reserving some of the potato.
Heat together the vegetables, eggs and sauce, and pour this into the potato border.
Pipe the remaining potato in lines over the filling, brush with beaten egg and bake at 400°F (200°C), Gas Mark 6, for 10-15 minutes, until the potato is lightly browned.

Potato Bangers

serves 4

1½ lb [750 g] **potatoes, sieved or riced**
½ oz [12.5 g] **butter**
1 egg, beaten
4 oz [100 g] **Cheddar cheese, finely grated**
2 teaspoons [2×5 ml spoons] **prepared English mustard**
8 thick beef sausages

Place the sausages under the grill to cook.
Add the butter, egg and cheese to the potatoes, beat well over a gentle heat till the cheese has melted.
Place in a piping bag fitted with a No. 10 star nozzle.
Cut each sausage lengthwise to allow it to open up and remain flat.
Spread each sausage with mustard to taste.
Pipe the potato mixture on the sausages to completely cover them.
Replace under the grill to allow potatoes to turn golden brown.

Potato, Bacon and Cottage Cheese Pudding

serves 4

1½ lb [750 g] **potatoes, parboiled for 15 minutes**
8 oz [250 g] **streaky bacon**
1 large onion, grated or finely chopped
1 lb [500 g] **cottage cheese**
3 eggs
sprigs of parsley to garnish
salt and pepper

Cut 1 lb (500 g) of the potatoes into thick slices and line a greased casserole with them.
Chop all but 3 rashers of the bacon and fry gently with the onion for 5 minutes.
Add to the cottage cheese and eggs in bowl and beat thoroughly.
Season and add to casserole.
Place the remaining potato slices round the edge, overlapping.
Stretch the remaining bacon rashers into rolls and decorate the top of the casserole with them.
Bake at 375°F (190°C), Gas Mark 5, for 35-40 minutes.

Scotch Potatoes

serves 4

1 lb [500 g] **Duchesse potato**
8 cooked chippolata sausages
egg and breadcrumbs

Divide the potato into 8 portions.
With floured hands, mould potato around each sausage and coat with egg and breadcrumbs.
Deep fry until golden brown and drain.
Serve either hot or cold.

Hazelnut and Potato Croquettes

serves 4

1 lb [500 g] **potatoes, mashed**
½ oz [12.5 g] **butter**
2 oz [50 g] **flour**
1 small onion, finely chopped
4 oz [100 g] **hazelnuts, roughly**
   chopped
½ teaspoon [2.5 ml] **basil**
oil
breadcrumbs
salt and pepper

Mash the potatoes with butter.
Add the flour, salt and pepper.
Fry the onion in a little oil until transparent.
Add to the potatoes with the nuts and basil and mix thoroughly.
Form into 10 croquettes, roll in breadcrumbs and fry until cooked and golden brown.

I love my Jean

I see her in the dewy flowers,
   I see her sweet and fair:
I hear her in the tunefu' birds,
   I hear her charm the air:
There's not a bony flower that
   springs
   By fountain, shaw, or green;
There's not a bony bird that
   sings,
   But minds me o' my Jean.

Robert Burns

Cheesy Upside Down

Apricot Drops

serves 4

8 oz [250 g] **potatoes, cooked, diced**
8 oz [250 g] **mixed vegetables of your choice, cooked**
8 oz can **tomatoes**
8 oz [250 g] **self raising flour**
a pinch of salt
3 oz [75 g] **butter**
1 egg
milk to mix
3 oz [75 g] **Cheddar cheese, grated**
salt and pepper

Place the potatoes and mixed vegetables in a buttered round ovenproof dish.
Pour over the tin of tomatoes and season with salt and pepper.
Sieve the flour into a bowl with a little salt, and rub in the butter.
Add the egg and sufficient milk to make a soft dough.
Roll out to size and place on top of the vegetables.
Brush with a little egg and milk and bake at 375°F (190°C), Gas Mark 5, for 30-35 minutes.
When cooked, turn out on to an ovenproof serving plate.
Sprinkle with grated cheese and return to the oven for a further 10 minutes to melt the cheese.

serves 4

8 oz [250 g] **potatoes, peeled**
8 oz [250 g] **bacon pieces**
1 onion, chopped
a pinch of sage
1 oz [25 g] **flour**
1 medium can apricot halves (8)
1 egg, beaten
fat for frying
salt and pepper
Sauce:
apricot juice from can
1 oz [25 g] **chopped walnuts**
arrowroot

Mince or finely chop the bacon.
Coarsely grate the potato, draining off all the excess moisture.
Mix together quickly the bacon, onion, flour, potatoes, sage and egg and seasoning to taste.
Drop dessertspoonfuls (10 ml spoons) of the mixture into deep fat and cook until golden brown.
Drain, place on a serving dish, topped with an apricot half.
A sauce can be served if desired. The juice from the can of apricots thickened with a little arrowroot, then add 1 oz (25 g) chopped walnuts and pour over the Apricot Drops.

The desire of all farmers is a good harvest and hopefully, as the proverb goes, 'a cold wet May means a barn full of hay' in the autumn.

Potato Macaroni

serves 4

8 oz [250 g] **potatoes, peeled and large diced**
3 oz [75 g] **macaroni, uncooked**
4 oz [100 g] **onions, peeled and sliced**
2 oz [50 g] **butter**
4 oz [100 g] **Cheddar cheese, grated**
¼ **pint** [125 ml] **milk**
salt and pepper

Place the potatoes in a pan with approximately 3 pints (1½ l) salted water.
Bring to the boil, add the macaroni, and cook till soft.
Gently fry the onion in the butter till golden, and remove from the pan.
Add the milk to the butter and bring to the boil.
Layer into a greased casserole the potatoes, macaroni and cheese, finishing with cheese.
Pour over the boiling milk and butter.
Place the onions on top and serve immediately.

Duchesse Meat Slice

serves 4

1 lb [500 g] **potatoes, sieved or riced**
1 oz [25 g] **butter**
1 **egg, beaten**
1 **small can pork luncheon meat**
2-3 **tomatoes**
apple chutney
salt and pepper

Add the butter and half the egg to the potatoes. Beat well and check seasoning.
Cut the meat into 4 slices lengthwise, then cut each slice in half.
Spread each slice with chutney.
Pipe or pile the potato on to each slice of meat.
Brush over with the remaining egg.
Garnish with slices of tomato and place on a greased baking sheet.
Bake at 450°F (230°C), Gas Mark 8, approx. 10 minutes until the potato is golden brown.

Cauliflower and Bacon Crisp

serves 4

19½ **oz packet of potato crisps**
1 **cauliflower**
2 oz [50 g] **butter**
8 oz [250 g] **streaky bacon**
1 **onion, sliced**
1 **packet cheese sauce mix**
½ **pint** [250 ml] **milk**
2 oz [50 g] **Cheddar cheese, grated**
salt and pepper

Cut the cauliflower into sprigs and cook in boiling water for 15 minutes.
Melt the butter and fry the bacon and onion for 4 minutes.
Prepare the sauce and add the cooked bacon and onion.
Pour the sauce over the cauliflower and cover with cheese and crumbled crisps.
Place under a hot grill to brown.

Spring

Whatever would happen, I wonder, if things didn't begin and end, come and go, rise and fall. If in the words of the song 'there'd be no more crying, no more dying, no more striving'. Heaven- they say. Would it, I wonder?

A life with no contrasts. A world all one colour. Roses all the year round and everyone smiling.

We'd go dotty with the monotony. And if, in a state of bliss with a blossom a-bloom and the summer breeze on our brow, we exclaim, 'If only this would go on for ever.' What a monstrous lie we tell.

The warmth of the sun is more luxurious for giving back what its absence has taken away. A greeting more joyful for being re-born

out of a parting with someone we love. Blossom more startling, born of a bare brown bough.

These are the contrasts which make up the balance of our lives, and add the colours - complementary one to the other - which turn everyday things into an exciting kaleidoscopic pattern of adventure.

Potato and Lentil Pie

serves 4

2 lb [1 kg] **potatoes**
1 oz [25 g] **butter**
a little hot milk
4 oz [100 g] **lentils**
1 onion
½ pint [250 ml] **stock or water**
3 oz [75 g] **Cheddar cheese, grated**
1 teaspoon [1×5 ml spoon]
parsley, chopped
1 oz [25 g] **butter**
½ teaspoon [2.5 ml] **meat extract**
salt and pepper

Soak the lentils overnight. Rinse
and simmer with the onion in the
water until tender. Drain.
Mix well with the cheese, parsley,
meat extract and seasoning.
Peel potatoes, and boil or steam.
Mash them well with butter,
seasoning and milk, to make a
fairly soft texture.
Butter a pie dish and spread with
some of the potato. Place the
lentil mixture on top and cover
with the remaining potato.
Mark with a fork.
Dot with butter and bake at
375°F (190°C), Gas Mark 5, for
30 minutes.

Meat and Potato Crisps

serves 4

6 oz [150 g] **potatoes, parboiled
for 5 minutes and grated**
12 oz [375 g] **beef, minced**
4 oz [100 g] **pork, minced**
1 onion, grated
3 oz [75 g] **cooked beetroot,
grated**
1 beaten egg
1 teaspoon [1×5 ml spoon]
vinegar
1 teaspoon [1×5 ml spoon]
parsley
oil
salt and pepper

Mix together the beef and pork
with onion and parsley.
Add the potatoes, beetroot, salt
and pepper and vinegar, and bind
with beaten egg.
Form into thin flat cakes and fry
over a gentle heat until brown and
crisp.

The blackthorn, or sloe, blossoms
early with white flowers, and later
bears a black, tart, flavoursome
fruit. The scattering of the ashes
of burned blackthorn over the
first sowings of spring was believed
to help produce an abundant
harvest.

And so, just as we're beginning
to tire of the smell of woodsmoke
and evenings by the fire which we
welcomed at the turn of the year,
we are ready to greet that
recognisable something on the air
which tells us it's spring.

Our hearts miss a beat - mine
does anyway. For this is the signal
to heave oneself out of the mental
hibernation into which endless
leaden skies and north-east winds
are apt to drive one, on the last
lap of winter.

I always think we must be a
little less of the human being in
the spring. A little closer to the
earth. For that indefinable something which we are all aware of
about now is akin, perhaps, to the
supersonic sound to which only
animal ears are sensitive?

Every year I say like the Irish,
'Next year I'll not be feelin' it.'
But next year is here; and spring
has struck again.

Barbara Hargreaves

Foiled Potato Parcel

Horse Brasses

Horse brasses have a long history, and derive from primitive m n's habit of hanging amulets on his animals, especially those he depended upon for cultivating his crops, or in battle.

It is for this reason that so many of brasses still carry primitive symbols, the Sun; the Wheel of the Sun; the Moon and Stars; and abstract geometrical designs having the same protective qualities. Other designs reflect the connection between the feudal vassal and his lord, with heraldic lions, eagles and griffins.

serves 4

1½ lb [750 g] tiny new potatoes
4 oz [100 g] mushrooms
4 oz [100 g] streaky bacon
2 oz [50 g] Cheddar cheese, grated
1 carton [5 fl oz or 125 ml] double cream
salt and pepper

Scrub or scrape the potatoes and place on a large sheet of aluminium foil.
Slice the mushrooms and bacon and place over the potatoes.
Season well and pour over the cream. Sprinkle with the cheese.
Make a secure parcel of the foil, and place on a baking sheet.
Bake at 375°F (190°C), Gas Mark 5, for about one hour.

Devilled Potatoes and Sausage

serves 4

1 lb [500 g] **new potatoes,**
   scraped and cooked
8 oz [250 g] **sliced sausage**
½ **oz** [12.5 g] **butter**
2½ **fl oz** [65 ml] **of single cream**
2 teaspoons [2×5 ml spoons]
   mustard
2 **tomatoes, sliced**
salt and pepper

Grill the sausage lightly.
Blend together the cream and mustard.
Toss the warm potatoes in melted butter and coat with the sauce.
Line the centre of the serving dish with the sausage, and surround with the devilled potatoes.
Garnish with sliced tomatoes.
Cooking time - 10 minutes.

Savoury Sausage and Mash

serves 4

1 lb [500 g] **potatoes, mashed**
1 **packet sage & onion stuffing,**
   reconstituted
8 oz [250 g] **tomatoes**
8 **pork sausages**
2 **rashers of bacon, with rind**
   removed
salt and pepper

Prepare the stuffing, chop the bacon and fry lightly.
Mix together the stuffing and potatoes and spread the mixture on to a greased ovenproof dish.
Slice the tomatoes and arrange in the centre of the potato mixture.
Place the sausages on the top and place in the oven for 30 minutes at 400°F (200°C), Gas Mark 6.

Bean and Bacon Cakes

serves 4

8 oz [250 g] **potatoes, mashed**
4 oz [100 g] **unsmoked bacon**
small can butter beans, drained
1 **level dessertspoon** [1×10 ml
   spoon] **flour**
1 **egg**
salt and pepper

Chop and fry the bacon.
Beat together the potatoes, butter beans, flour and egg then add the bacon and also any bacon fat left in the frying pan.
Place dessertspoonfuls of the mixture into the frying pan, shaping them into little patties.
Fry gently for 5 minutes on each side until golden brown. Serve with fried eggs.

Does it matter with which stick you beat your cattle? Apparently the ash keeps evil away and can never hurt the animal by which it is struck.

Farm-House Tasties

Potato Pancakes

serves 4

8 oz [250 g] **potatoes, peeled and grated**
8 oz [250 g] **pork sausage meat**
1 small onion, grated
1 apple, peeled and grated
1 egg, beaten
salt and pepper

Drain away any excess moisture from the potatoes.
Mix in the sausage meat, onion and apple, and bind together with the egg.
Fry in small spoonfuls in shallow fat, turning during cooking - about 7-8 minutes per side.
Drain on absorbent kitchen paper and serve piping hot.

Children's Favourite Potato and Cheese Pie

serves 4

5 good sized potatoes, cooked sieved or riced
2 oz [50 g] **Cheddar cheese, grated**
2 oz [50 g] **butter**
grated nutmeg
2 eggs, beaten
salt and pepper

Add the cheese, butter, salt and pepper, nutmeg and eggs to the potatoes and beat well.
Place the mixture in a well greased pie dish which is large enough to allow the mixture to rise.
Bake in a hot oven 400°F (200°C), Gas Mark 6, for 20 minutes.
Serve with tomato sauce.

serves 4

1 lb [500 g] **potatoes, peeled**
4 oz [100 g] **flour**
2 eggs
a little over ½ **pint** [250 ml] **milk**
2 tablespoons [2×20 ml spoons] **onion, grated**
2 tablespoons [2×20 ml spoons] **butter**
1 teaspoon [1×5 ml spoon] **salt**

Place the flour and salt in a bowl.
Beat the milk and eggs together and gradually beat into the flour.
Fry the onion in butter until it is transparent, but not coloured, and add to the batter.
Grate the potatoes directly into the batter and blend well.
Cook spoonfuls on a lightly greased frying pan or in an omelette pan, cooking on each side.
The pancakes can then be filled with meat or fish, in a thick sauce.

Potato and Onion Cake

serves 4

1½ lb [750 g] **potatoes, peeled and cooked**
1 **egg**
3 **medium onions, sliced**
1 oz [25 g] **butter**
4 oz [100 g] **Cheddar cheese, grated**

Mash the potato until creamy with butter, egg and milk, and add the salt and pepper.
Fry the onion in the butter until golden brown.
Spread half the potato mixture into an 8 inch (20 cm) sandwich tin.
Place the onions and half the cheese on top of the potato and then spread the remaining potato over and smooth flat.
Sprinkle with the remaining cheese.
Bake in a hot oven 400°F (200°C), Gas Mark 6, for 30-40 minutes until golden brown. If the cake is to be turned out, line the tin with greaseproof paper, or use a non-stick tin.

Potato and Bacon Cakes

serves 4

1 lb [500 g] **potatoes, sieved or riced**
3 oz [75 g] **bacon, chopped**
1 **medium onion, finely chopped**
1 teaspoon [1×5 ml spoon] **meat or vegetable extract**
1 level tablespoon [1×20 ml spoon] **parsley, chopped**
milk
breadcrumbs
fat for frying
salt and pepper

Place the bacon in a pan over a gentle heat to allow the fat to run. Add the onion and fry till golden brown.
Mix together the potatoes, bacon and onion, extract and seasoning and parsley.
Form into 8 cakes, using floured hands.
Brush with milk and roll in breadcrumbs.
Fry in a little hot fat to brown on both sides, or in a moderately hot oven, 350°F (180°C), Gas Mark 4, till firm.

Egg and Potato Hotch-Pot

serves 4

1 lb [500 g] **potatoes, peeled and boiled**
8 oz [250 g] **tomatoes, peeled and chopped**
4 oz [100 g] **mushrooms, washed and sliced**
4 oz [100 g] **courgettes, washed and sliced**
4 **eggs**
2 oz [50 g] **butter**
4 oz [100 g] **Cheddar cheese, grated**
a few onion rings
salt and pepper

Fry the courgettes lightly in the butter. Add the potatoes, tomatoes and mushrooms and cook for a further 5 minutes. Season.
Whisk up the eggs, add half the cheese and blend in the vegetables.
Pour into a greased ovenproof dish, cover with the remaining grated cheese and bake at 350°F (180°C), Gas Mark 4, for 20-30 minutes.
Serve garnished with raw onion rings.

If butterflies appear in early spring, or the oak comes into leaf before the ash, then it will be a good summer.

If the onions have an extra skin, or the husks on the corn are thicker than usual, or the squirrels store more food, then it will be a hard winter.

Florida Potatoes

serves 4

1 lb [500 g] **new potatoes, cooked**
1 small can **pineapple chunks**
5 oz [125 g] **cottage cheese**
8 oz [250 g] **chicken or ham cooked**
1 head of **chicory**
paprika pepper
salt and pepper

Cut the potatoes into dice.
Drain the juice from the pineapple.
Add the pineapple chunks, cottage cheese and meat (cut into cubes) to the potatoes and blend gently together.
Separate the leaves of chicory, wash well and drain.
Arrange on a round plate, radiating from the centre.
Place the potato mixture in the centre and sprinkle lightly with paprika pepper.

Bacon and Potato Patties

serves 4

1½ lb [750 g] **potatoes, cooked**
4 oz [100 g] **bacon, rind removed and diced**
1 **egg, beaten**
salt and pepper

Mash the potatoes well and blend in the egg.
Add seasoning to taste.
Lightly fry the bacon then mix together the bacon and potatoes and shape into patties on a floured board.
Fry in shallow fat, turning until golden brown.

Curried Potato Cutlets

serves 4

12 oz [375 g] **potato, cooked and sieved**
8 oz [250 g] **cooked minced meat**
3 or 4 tablespoons [3 or 4×20 ml spoons] **thick curry sauce**
fat for frying
Coating:
beaten egg
fine oatmeal
1 **lemon**

Mix together the potato, meat, and enough sauce and seasoning to bind the mixture.
Form into cutlets and coat with egg and oatmeal.
Fry in hot fat on both sides.
Serve garnished with lemon butterflies.

Cottage Cheese Flan

serves 4

1 lb [500 g] **potatoes, cooked and diced**
1 lb [500 g] **cottage cheese**
4-5 fl oz [100-125 ml] **fresh sour cream**
8 oz [250 g] **shortcrust pastry**
chives or parsley, chopped
salt and pepper

Press the cottage cheese through a sieve or liquidise.
Add the cream and mix well together (if very dry add a little more cream).
Fold in the potatoes and season with salt and pepper.
Line a 9 inch (23 cm) flan ring with pastry and fill with the cheese mixture.
Bake at 350°F (180°C), Gas Mark 4 for approx. 45 minutes until brown.
Garnish with chives or parsley.
It is better to allow the flan to cool very slightly before serving.

The oak is the king of trees, flowering in midsummer. Its roots were believed to mirror underground its lofty branches, symbolising endurance and triumph, and the ruler of both Heaven and Hades.

Potato and Ham Crunch

serves 4

1 lb [500 g] **potatoes, cooked and diced**
1 packet **potato crisps**
2 large **onions, skinned and diced**
4 hard boiled **eggs, diced**
4 slices of **ham**
½ pint [250 ml] **cheese sauce**
4 oz [100 g] **flour**
2 oz [50 g] **butter**
2 oz [50 g] **Cheddar cheese, grated**

Sauté the onions in the butter, add the potatoes and turn into a greased ovenproof dish.
Cover with the sauce then place the ham over the top.
Rub the fat into the flour, stir in the cheese and crushed crisps.
Sprinkle over the ham and bake at 400°F (200°C), Gas Mark 6, for 30-40 minutes until golden brown.

Dip for New Potatoes

serves 4

8 oz [250 g] **Cheddar cheese, mature**
1 small can **evaporated milk**
1 teaspoon [1×5 ml spoon] **dry mustard**
1 **egg, beaten**
4 tablespoons [4×20 ml spoons] **white wine, dry**
salt and pepper

Cut the cheese into small pieces and place in a bowl over water.
Add the evaporated milk and cook till the cheese is melted.
Remove from the heat, add the mustard, egg, salt and pepper, and stir well.
Add the wine, return to the heat, but do not boil.
Dip potatoes into the dunk with a cocktail stick.

Country Classics Bibliography

Whatever your interests are, begin with the classics. Izaak Walton's 'Compleat Angler', composite of fishing conversation, moralising and cookery. Gilbert White's 'Natural History and Antiquities of Selbourne', meticulous observation, particularly of birds. William Cobbett's 'Rural Rides', the countryside through the eyes of a journalist and politician. Fascinating for comparison with today. Richard Jeffries appealing to the heart and senses, 'Bevis' about a small boy in the country; 'Hodge and his Masters', about 19th century country social life. Jeffries and Henry Williamson have much in common. 'Tarka the Otter', 'The Old Stag', 'Salar the Salmon', 'The Peregrine Saga', 'The Phasian Bird' and the

Savoy Patties

serves 4

8 oz [250 g] **potatoes, sieved or riced**
8 oz [250 g] **cooked cabbage, finely chopped**
4 oz [100 g] **pork luncheon meat, shredded and diced**
1 teaspoon [1×5 ml spoon] **onion, grated**
1 **egg, beaten**
a little **cooking oil**
salt and pepper

Blend together the potatoes, cabbage, meat, onion and egg. Season.
Shape into patties, using a floured board.
Heat sufficient oil in pan, barely covering the base, add the patties and cook over a low heat till golden brown on both sides.

Potato Bacon Hash

serves 4

1½ lb [750 g] **potatoes, peeled and cooked**
1 **onion, skinned**
4-6 oz [100-150 g] **streaky bacon**
2 tablespoons [2×20 ml spoons] **milk**
1 oz [25 g] **flour**
1 oz [25 g] **butter**
salt and pepper

Cut the potatoes into small dice.
Chop the onion finely, then dice the bacon.
Make a batter, using the milk and flour, season well, then mix all the ingredients together.
Grease a baking tin and spread in the mixture.
Bake at 450°F (230°C), Gas Mark 8, for 20 minutes until pale golden brown.

Sweetcorn and Bacon Potatoes

serves 4

1 lb [500 g] **potatoes, peeled and parboiled**
8 oz [250 g] **bacon, rind removed, and chopped**
1 large **onion, peeled and chopped**
1 can of **corn kernels**
3 **eggs**
salt and pepper

Slice the potatoes and place in the bottom of a greased pie dish.
Fry the bacon and onion lightly until cooked, and then add the sweet corn.
Cover the potatoes with the bacon mixture and pour the lightly beaten eggs, seasoned, over the top.
Bake at 375°F (190°C), Gas Mark 5, for 30 minutes, until set and lightly browned.

'Story of a Norfolk Farm' - all good country reading.

George Borrow's rather heavy 'lavengro' fills in the facts of 19th century gipsy life. Hilliare Belloc's essays 'Hills and the Sea' about the South country rate as first class, with W.H. Hudson's 'Impressions of a Shepherds Life' about Salisbury Plain.

Robert Gibbings in our time wrote 'Sweet Thames Run Softly', 'Lovely is the Lee', and 'Coming Down the Wye' from source to estuary with lovely woodcuts.

Gavin Maxwell's 'Ring of Bright Water', and T.H. White's 'The Goshawk' and Rowena Farre's 'Seal Morning' are superlative on living with wild creatures. Adrian Bell's 'Corduroy', Laurie Lee's 'Cider with Rosie and Flora Thompson's 'Lark Rise to Candleford' and Ronald Blythe's 'Akenfield' are fine on village and country life.

The old Badminton Series if available are marvellous on all country sports from Foxhunting and Shooting to Polo. Observer series are perfect for the identification of anything. Collins very detailed 'New Naturalist' series is the best I know. Batsfords and Witherbys are two more publishers who specialise in country books.

Tatie Pot

serves 4

1 lb [500 g] **potatoes**
1 lb [500 g] **neck of lamb**
8 oz [250 g] **black pudding**
1 large onion
½ pint [250 ml] **stock**
salt and pepper

Peel and slice the vegetables.
Cube the lamb and black
pudding.
Layer the vegetable mixture and
the meat mixture in a deep,
straight sided casserole dish,
seasoning each layer, and
finishing with vegetables.
Pour over the hot stock, cover and
bake at 375°F (190°C), Gas
Mark 5, for 1½ hours.
Remove the lid and cook for a
further ½ hour at 400°F (200°C),
Gas Mark 6, to brown the
potatoes.
Traditionally, this is served with
pickled red cabbage.

Potato Race

A running contest, where the
winner is the first who collects in a
basket or other receptacle a
number of potatoes, usually eight,
placed, as a rule two yards apart,
along a straight line, and then
crosses a finish line five or ten
yards further on.

Encyclopaedia Brittannica 1911

Potato Rings

serves 4

1 lb [500 g] **potatoes, peeled**
sage and onion stuffing
1 egg, beaten
fat for frying
salt

Remove the centre of the potatoes
with an apple corer and slice
thinly.
Dip slices into the egg, then into
the stuffing.
Fry very gently till the potato is
cooked.

Horse-Radish Salad

serves 4

1 lb [500 g] **potatoes, boiled and**
diced
1 large onion, skinned and
chopped
a few sprigs of mint, chopped
1 small carton soured cream
2 tablespoons [2 × 20 ml spoons]
horse-radish sauce
8 slices of cold roast beef
a little parsley, chopped

Parboil the potatoes for 4-5
minutes.
Mix together with the onion,
mint, soured cream and
horse-radish.
Place spoonfuls of the mixture
inside each slice of beef and roll
up.
Pile left over salad mixture on an
oval platter, place beef rolls on
top and garnish with chopped
parsley.

Leek, Egg and Potato Nests

serves 4

1 lb [500 g] **potatoes, boiled and**
sieved or riced
3 leeks, trimmed and sliced
1½ oz [37 g] **butter**
4 eggs, boiled for 6 minutes
salt and black pepper
Sauce:
2½ fl oz [65 ml] **fresh sour cream**
1 tablespoon [1 × 20 ml spoon]
H.P. sauce
1 spring onion, finely chopped
3 oz [75 g] **Cheddar cheese,**
grated
½ teaspoon [2.5 ml] **lemon juice**
salt and black pepper

Cook the leeks gently in butter
and when cooked add to the
potatoes with salt and black
pepper.
Mix well together.
Divide the mixture into four, and
place in individual greased
ramekin dishes. With a fork,
work the mixture up the sides of
the dish to form a nest.
Cut the eggs in two lengthwise,
and place in the dish.
Mix all the sauce ingredients
together and spoon over each
nest.
Place in a hot oven and bake at
375°F (190°C), Gas Mark 5, for
25 minutes.

Rémoulade of Potatoes

serves 4

1 lb [500 g] **potatoes, boiled**
1 small can anchovy fillets
1 dessertspoon [1×10 ml spoon]
   capers
2 oz [50 g] **black olives**
¼ pint [125 ml] **mayonnaise**
a little tomato purée to colour

Cut the potatoes into small dice
and place in a bowl.
Drain the oil from the anchovies
and chop finely. (Household
scissors are best)
Add the potatoes with the capers,
pitted and chopped olives.
Blend with coloured mayonnaise.
Serve with crisp lettuce leaves.

Potatoes with Sour Cream

serves 4

1 lb [500 g] **potatoes, peeled**
2 tablespoons [2×20 ml spoons]
   butter
1 tablespoon [1×20 ml spoon]
   chives
1 carton soured cream
salt and pepper

Peel the potatoes thinly, and cook
in salted water until just cooked.
Drain, and cut them into dice.
Melt the butter in a frying pan,
brown the potatoes in the fat,
then season.
Add the chives, soured cream,
and cover, then allow to simmer
over a low heat until all the cream
is absorbed.
Serve hot as an accompaniment to
cold meat dishes, or fish.

Thoughts on a May Morning

You need to be young to smell
   daisies,
    Or tell what the whitethroat
   sings.
You need to be young to catch
   sunbeams,
    Or soar on the skylark's wings.

You need to be young to taste
   hawthorn,
    Or hear how the bluebell rings.
You need to be young to count
   swallows,
    Or know what the cuckoo
   brings.

You need to be young to seek
   rainbows
    Or notice the tiny things.
You need to be young to know
   wonder,
    Young as a million springs!

Beryl Ralph

Egg and Mayonnaise Salad

serves 4

8 oz [250 g] **new potatoes, cooked and diced**
4 **hard boiled eggs**
½ **cucumber, diced**
2 or 3 **raw carrots**
3-4 oz [75-100 g] **Cheddar cheese, small diced**
8 teaspoons [8×5 ml spoons] **mayonnaise**
lettuce leaves
French dressing

Mix together the potatoes, cucumber, carrots and cheese with some oil and vinegar dressing and spread in a flat dish garnished with crisp lettuce leaves.
Halve the eggs and stand them rounded side up in two rows on the bed of vegetables.
Top each egg with a teaspoonful of mayonnaise and sprinkle alternately with chopped parsley and paprika pepper.

Windfall Salad

serves 4

1 lb [500 g] **small new potatoes, scraped**
2 **eating apples, cored**
2 **sticks celery**
8 oz [250 g] **fresh cherries, stoned**
½ **a pear, cored**
1×4 oz [100 g] **carton cottage cheese**
3 tablespoons [3×20 ml spoons] **single cream**
a few sprigs of mint

Cook the potatoes in boiling salted water, and whilst these are cooking prepare the other ingredients.
Dice the apples and pear, chop the celery, and cut the cherries in half.
Drain the potatoes and whilst they are still warm, mix together with all the other ingredients.
Leave to chill for 1-2 hours.
Garnish with sprigs of mint.

British Farm Horses

Since mechanisation overtook us all the numbers of farm and draught horses have declined dramatically, but a few enthusiasts have kept the breeds going and some farmers retained just one horse for odd jobs. Some brewers have kept splendid teams and use them successfully for local deliveries. Now numbers increase as farmers find that for some jobs and on some soils, the horse is again an economic proposition as costs of machinery and fuels continue to soar.

First recorded in about 1506 the Suffolk Punch was developed on the East Suffolk coast. Standing 15-16 hands, this bright chestnut horse with clean legs (little hair or feather) was the first type to replace draught oxen for agricultural work. During the 15th century horses got smaller and in 1541, Henry VIII enacted a statute to reverse this trend and imported some good Flemish mares eventually to produce the 'Great Horse of England', the Shire bred mainly in Lincoln, Cambridge and Huntingdon. Slow moving but tough, Shire horses stand 17 hands and over and can pull a net weight of 5 tons.

The Percheron has clean feet and is always grey or black, dappled white, stands over 16 hands and has an immensely strong body on shortish legs. He is active and capable of pulling enormous weights.

Clydesdales were developed in Lanarkshire in Scotland during the 18th century, mainly as commercial draught horses, although many were and are used on farms. Clydesdales have characteristically good action and may be bay, brown or black with a lot of white on face and feathered legs. They have plenty of quality and weight without being quite so bulky as the other breeds.

Hot Potato Salad

serves 4

2 lb [1 kg] **new potatoes, scrubbed**
1 oz [25 g] **butter or bacon fat**
1 teaspoon [1×5 ml spoon] **flour**
¼ **cup of vinegar**
½ **cup of water, reserved from potatoes**
4 **spring onions**
4 **rashers streaky bacon, crisply fried**
1 tablespoon [1×20 ml spoon] **parsley, chopped**
1 tablespoon [1×20 ml spoon] **sugar**
1 teaspoon [1×5 ml spoon] **salt**

Cook the potatoes in boiling, salted water until just tender.
Drain them and reserve ½ a cup of the liquor.
Melt the fat or butter in a pan, stir in the flour and salt, and cook for a minute without colouring.
Add the water, vinegar, onion and sugar gradually, stirring continuously and bring to the boil.
Add the potatoes and chopped bacon.
Cover with a lid and place over a gentle heat for 15 minutes, shaking the pan occasionally.
Place in a serving dish and garnish with parsley.

Potato Egg Savoury

serves 4

1 lb [500 g] **new potatoes, cooked**
4 oz [100 g] **Cheddar cheese, grated**
4 **spring onions, sliced**
2 **large tomatoes, sliced**
2 **eggs**
¼ **pint [125 ml] milk**
½ oz [12.5 g] **butter**
1 teaspoon [1×5 ml spoon] **made mustard**
parsley
salt and pepper

Grease an ovenproof dish with butter.
Slice the potatoes to ¼ inch (0.5 cm) thick and place in a dish with alternate layers of cheese, onions and tomatoes, finishing with cheese.
Beat the eggs with milk, mustard and seasoning and pour into the dish.
Bake at 375°F (190°C), Gas Mark 5, until the custard is set and the top is golden brown - about 40-45 minutes.
Garnish with parsley.

Potato Cauliflower au Gratin

serves 4

1 lb [500 g] **potatoes**
1 **good sized cauliflower**
Sauce:
1 oz [25 g] **butter**
1 oz [25 g] **plain flour**
¼ **pint [125 ml] milk**
¼ **pint [125 ml] water from the cauliflower**
a pinch of mustard
3 oz [75 g] **Cheddar cheese, grated**
paprika pepper
salt and pepper

Peel and dice the potatoes.
Break the cauliflower into small sprigs, including some of the green leaves.
Place together in boiling, salted water and cook until just tender.
Drain well and reserve ¼ pint (125 ml) of the stock.
Sauce:
Melt the butter and cook the flour in it for 2 minutes.
Stir in the milk and stock and cook until thick.
Add the seasoning to taste, and most of the cheese.
Combine the vegetables and sauce and pour into a buttered dish.
Sprinkle with the remaining cheese.
Grill or bake in a hot oven 425°F (220°C), Gas Mark 7, until brown.
Garnish with paprika.

Potato Ratatouille

serves 4

8-12 oz [250-375 g] **potatoes cooked**
2 **large onions**
2 **cloves garlic**
4 **tablespoons** [4×20 ml spoons] **olive oil**
3 **large tomatoes, ripe**
2 **peppers, red or green**
4 **courgettes**
1 **tablespoon** [1×20 ml spoon] **parsley, finely chopped**
pinch oregano
salt and freshly ground black pepper

Peel and thinly slice the onions and divide them into rings.
Crush the garlic.
Remove the core and seeds of the peppers and cut the flesh into thin strips.
Cover the tomatoes with boiling water, leave to stand for two minutes and then slide off the skins. Chop the tomatoes roughly.
Cut the courgettes and potatoes into small cubes.
Heat the olive oil in a deep frying pan.
Add the onions and garlic and cook over a very low heat until the onions are transparent and pale yellow.
Add the peppers and cook for a further 10 minutes until soft.
Add the courgettes and tomatoes, season with salt and freshly ground black pepper, cover and simmer for 20 minutes.
Add the potatoes, the parsley and oregano, stir gently, and cook for a further 10 minutes.

Essex Salad

serves 4

1 **lb** [500 g] **potatoes, cooked and diced**
¼ **pint** [125 ml] **mayonnaise**
2 **oz** [50 g] **walnuts, chopped**
1 **onion, diced**
2 **carrots, diced**
1 **green pepper, diced, or green peas**
cabbage leaves or lettuce
1 **tomato, sliced**

Mix the potato, the mayonnaise, chopped nuts, diced carrots, onion and peas.
Line a salad bowl with cabbage leaves or lettuce and pile the salad into the centre.
Garnish with sliced tomatoes and green pepper rings.
Variations:
Diced cooked meat
Chopped shrimps
Chopped hard boiled eggs and anchovies.

Mimosa Potatoes

serves 4

1 **lb** [500 g] **potatoes, small**
2 **hard boiled eggs**
1 **oz** [25 g] **butter**

Peel the potatoes and steam or boil them. Drain them well and replace the pan over a very low heat to make the potatoes floury.
Sieve the eggs or chop them very finely, then stir them into the melted butter in a pan.
Serve the potatoes covered with the egg mixture.
Garnish with a little freshly chopped parsley.

Spinach Pie

serves 4

Pastry:
8 **oz** [250 g] **potatoes, sieved or riced**
4 **oz** [100 g] **plain flour**
2 **oz** [50 g] **butter**
½ **teaspoon** [2.5 ml] **baking powder**
a pinch of salt
water to mix
Filling:
2 **lb** [1 kg] **fresh spinach**
4 **oz** [100 g] **Parmesan cheese**
2 **eggs, beaten**
3 **oz** [75 g] **ham or bacon, chopped (optional)**
ground black pepper
salt

Pastry:
Rub the fat into the flour till it resembles fine breadcrumbs.
Add the baking powder and salt, then the potatoes, and blend thoroughly.
Add sufficient water to form a stiff dough.
With 2/3 of the pastry, line a greased tin.
Boil the spinach till cooked.
Drain well and allow to get cold, then squeeze so that no water remains.
Place in a mixing bowl with the Parmesan cheese, pepper and eggs and mix well together.
Place in the tin, and then add the ham or bacon if used.
Cover with the remaining pastry, sealing the edge with water and flute up with the fingers.
Make two slits in the centre of the pastry.
Bake in a moderate oven at 350°F (180°C), Gas Mark 4, for approx. 30-35 minutes, till golden brown.

Why is a horseshoe a lucky symbol to hang above your door? Because it is made of iron - a metal that traditionally repels witches; it is shaped somewhat like the lucky new moon; it contains the lucky number of seven nails; and horses themselves symbolise heroism and virility. But be sure to hang the horseshoe the right way, with its points uppermost, so that your luck cannot fall out.

Is it going to rain? Then look for jackdaws fluttering round buildings and for cows lying down on low ground; and listen for crickets loudly chirping, roosters crowing from gates, cats sneezing, and the restless bleating of sheep.

Sauté Spring Potatoes

serves 4

1½ **lb** [750 g] **tiny new potatoes, cooked or cut into slices ½ inch [1 cm] thick**
1 **bunch of spring onions, chopped**
1 **oz** [25 g] **butter**
2 **teaspoons** [2×5 ml spoons] **mustard powder**
salt and pepper

Melt the butter in a pan, and add the potatoes and onions, then sprinkle with mustard powder.
Sauté till the potatoes are golden, turning frequently.

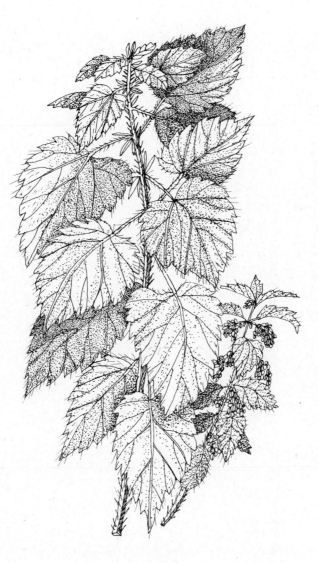

The Stinging Nettle

Golden Potatoes

serves 4

12 **oz** [750 g] **new potatoes**
1 **onion**
2 **oz** [50 g] **butter**
4 **tablespoons** [4×20 ml spoons] **fresh sour cream**
parsley, chopped
salt and pepper

Cook the potatoes in boiling salted water.
Chop the onion finely and fry in the butter for 5 minutes.
Dice the potatoes and add to the pan and toss with the onion until the potatoes turn golden.
Season to taste and stir in the cream.
Cook very gently until the cream bubbles.
Serve hot, garnished with parsley.

This is a familiar weed which has been well-known to country cooks for centuries: the young tops when about 6″ high are boiled like spinach and have a pleasant earthy taste.
From Scotland comes a recipe for nettle pudding made with leeks or onions, cabbage and rice all boiled in a muslin bag and traditionally served with butter or gravy.
Nettle beer and nettle tea were once familiar country drinks.
In addition to its culinary uses dried nettles can be fed to livestock - few animals will eat the growing plant.
In war-time nettle fibres have been used for making textiles.

Nanette Potatoes

serves 4

1 lb [500 g] **new potatoes**
1 oz [25 g] **butter**
2 tablespoons [2×20 ml spoons]
   flour
1 pint [500 ml] **stock**
nutmeg
parsley
salt and pepper

Wash and scrape new potatoes
and leave in cold water until
required.
Melt butter in a saucepan, add
flour and stir well until a good
brown roux is achieved.
Add stock slowly, stirring all the
time.
Add salt and a pinch of nutmeg.
Bring gently to the boil, and add
the potatoes and two sprigs of
parsley.
Cover the saucepan and cook very
slowly until tender.
Serve hot.

Pommes Marquise

serves 4

1 lb [500 g] **Duchesse potato**
some sliced, skinned tomato
1 oz [25 g] **butter**

Pipe the potato on to a greased tin
in the shape of cottage loaves.
Make a slight hollow with the
thumb in each one, put in
chopped tomatoes.
Brush with melted butter and
bake at 400°F (200°C), Gas Mark
6, for 8-10 minutes.

Mixed Vegetable Curry

serves 4

1 lb [500 g] **tiny new potatoes**
½ **medium size cauliflower**
8 oz [250 g] **carrots**
4 celery stalks, large
½ pint [250 ml] **curry sauce**
6 oz [150 g] **Cheddar cheese,**
   grated
salt

Slice the potatoes and carrots
thinly. Divide the cauliflower into
florets and chop the celery.
Cook the vegetables in boiling
salted water till tender. Drain and
place in an ovenproof dish.
Add the curry sauce and heat.
Pour into a greased ovenproof
dish and sprinkle with grated
cheese.
Flash under a hot grill until the
cheese bubbles.

Curry Sauce:
½ oz [12.5 g] **butter**
½ oz [12.5 g] **flour**
½ pint [250 ml] **stock from**
   vegetables
1 teaspoon [1×5 ml spoon]
   concentrated curry sauce

Make a paste of flour and water.
Mix all together and stir until
mixture boils and thickens.

Leek and Potato Savoury

serves 4

1 lb [500 g] **potatoes, peeled**
2 leeks, sliced
1 oz [25 g] **butter**
1 packet parsley sauce
fresh parsley
salt and pepper

Cut the potatoes into even sizes
and cook until tender.
Melt the butter in a pan and fry
the leeks.
Make up the parsley sauce as
directed and add the leeks.
Pour over the cooked potatoes
and garnish with freshly chopped
parsley.
Serve with cold meats.

Deep Fried Fritters

serves 4

1 large potato
1 large cooking apple
2 egg whites
fat for frying
a pinch of cinnamon
salt

Peel the potato and grate, pouring
off the excess water.
Peel the apple, remove the core
and grate into the potato.
Add the cinnamon and salt.
Whisk the egg whites stiffly and
fold into the potato and apple.
Fry spoonfuls in hot, deep fat till
golden brown.
Serve with ham or pork.

Summertime Medley

serves 4

1 lb [500 g] **new potatoes**
6 spring onions
2 oz [50 g] **butter**
a good pinch sugar
1 cup water or stock
8 oz [250 g] **fresh peas (or small**
 packet frozen peas)
2 outside lettuce leaves, shredded
1 teaspoon [1×5 ml spoon]
 cornflour
salt and pepper

Scrape the potatoes and slice to
¼ inch (0.5 cm) thick. Leave
whole if they are small.
Wash and trim the spring onions.
Melt the butter in a pan and fry
the onions and potatoes for 5
minutes without colouring.
Stir in cornflour, sugar and
seasoning, and cook for 1 minute.
Add the water, cover and cook for
10 minutes, or until the potatoes
are nearly tender.
Add the peas and shredded
lettuce and cook for a further 5
minutes. Do not overcook at this
stage. Adjust seasoning.
Serve immediately.

Lately there has been a revival
of interest in corn dollies - attractive figures and shapes imagina-
tively woven from stalks of grain.
Now examples of a folk art form,
once these fertility symbols were
considered potent sources of
magic, stemming from the God-
dess Ceres, designed to increase
the bounty of the harvest.

Hot Potato and Raisin Salad

serves 4

1½ lb [750 g] **tiny new potatoes**
2 tablespoons [2×20 ml spoons] **olive oil**
1 tablespoon [1×20 ml spoon] **white wine vinegar**
1 teaspoon [1×5 ml spoon] **paprika**
1 teaspoon [1×5 ml spoon] **tobasco sauce**
1 tablespoon [1×20 ml spoon] **tomato purée**
2 tablespoons [2×20 ml spoons] **seedless raisins**
salt and pepper

Place the potatoes in boiling salted water and cook till just tender. Drain well.
Blend together the oil, vinegar, paprika, sauce, purée and season.
Stir in the raisins and allow to stand for ½ hour.
Place the dressing in a pan with the potatoes and warm over a gentle heat.

Potato and Lentil Goulash

serves 4

1 lb [500 g] **potato, peeled and boiled**
3 oz [75 g] **(dry weight) lentils, soaked overnight**
1 large onion, skinned and chopped
1 medium can of tomatoes
2 tablespoons [2×20 ml spoons] **tomato purée**
1 tablespoon [1×20 ml spoon] **Worcestershire sauce**
1 oz [25 g] **butter**
2 oz [50 g] **grated cheese**
1 carton soured cream
salt and pepper

Slice the potatoes thickly.
Fry the onion lightly, and add the tomato, tomato purée, sauce, and then stir in the sour cream.
Season.
Line the bottom of a greased ovenproof dish with potatoes, then arrange alternate layers of soaked lentils and cooked potatoes.
Pour over the tomato mixture and sprinkle the top with finely grated cheese.
Cook in the hot oven at 375°F (190°C), Gas Mark 5, for 30-40 minutes.

Leek and Potato Hotpot

serves 4

1 lb [500 g] **potatoes, peeled and sliced**
2 medium sized leeks, cut in pieces
1 tablespoon [1×20 ml spoon] **flour**
1 oz [25 g] **butter**
½ **pint** [250 ml] **milk**
salt and pepper

Arrange a layer of potatoes and leeks in a greased ovenproof dish.
Sprinkle with a little flour, season with salt and pepper, and dot with a few butter pats.
Continue till all the vegetables are used, finishing with a layer of potatoes.
Dot with remaining butter, add the milk, and cover the dish with a lid or foil.
Cook at 325°F (170°C), Gas Mark 3, for one hour, then remove lid and cook for a further ½ hour till the potatoes are golden brown.

Stuffed Tomatoes

serves 4

8 good sized tomatoes
Stuffing:
6 oz [150 g] **potato, sieved**
2 oz [50 g] **cheese, grated**
½ oz [12.5 g] **melted butter**
a little milk or beaten egg
a pinch of mustard salt and pepper
fat for frying
2 slices bread, halved

Stand the tomatoes on the stalk end and slice the top from each one.
Scoop out the pulp with a teaspoon.
Mix all the ingredients for the filling, season to taste, and moisten with the tomato pulp.
Pipe the potato through a forcing bag to fill each tomato and make a rosette above it. Replace the lids.
Place in a lightly greased dish and bake at 375°F (190°C), Gas Mark 5, for about 15 minutes.
Serve on rounds of fried bread.

Growing Pains

I've planted stocks,
    I've planted phlox
Sometimes they grow,
    sometimes they don't
I've planted lots
    Of young shallots,
Sometimes they will,
    Sometimes they won't
Upon my knees
    I've planted peas,
Some of them thrive,
    But not the rest,
One thing stands out
    Beyond all doubt -
The wretched weeds
    Still grow the best.

Soufflé of Potatoes and Carrots

serves 4

8 oz [250 g] **potatoes, sieved or riced**
1 large onion, finely chopped
1 lb [500 g] **carrots, scraped**
1 level teaspoon [1×5 ml spoon] **dried mixed herbs**
2 large eggs
knob of butter
salt and pepper

Boil the carrots with the onions till very tender, and drain well.
Mash well or liquidise.
Add the potatoes and the herbs.
Separate the eggs, and add the yolks to the mixture, with butter, and beat well together.
Beat the egg whites till very stiff and fold into the mixture using a metal spoon.
Place in a buttered soufflé dish and cook at 375°F (190°C), Gas Mark 5, for 25-30 minutes till well risen and golden brown.
Serve at once.

Sweet and Sour New Potatoes

serves 4

1 lb [500 g] **new potatoes, scraped**
1 level teaspoon [1×5 ml spoon] **cornflour**
1 tablespoon [1×20 ml spoon] **water**
1 tablespoon [1×20 ml spoon] **vinegar**
1 tablespoon [1×20 ml spoon] **sugar**
1 tablespoon [1×20 ml spoon] **soy sauce**
1 oz [25 g] **flaked almonds, toasted**
salt and pepper

Cook the potatoes in boiling salted water for 15-20 minutes, then drain.
Blend together the cornflour and water, then place in a small pan with the sugar, vinegar and soy sauce; bring to the boil.
Add the potatoes to the sauce and stir gently until they are coated.
Serve sprinkled with toasted flaked almonds.

E.T.S.

Green Pepper and Potato Bake

Ticknor Edwardes in The Lore of the Honey Bee tells us that, contrary to popular belief, 'the queen-bee is the very reverse of a monarch, both by nature and inclination. She possesses only the merest rudiments of intelligence. She has a magnificent body, great docility, certain almost unrestrainable impulses and passions, a yielding womanish love of the yoke; but she is incapable of action other than that arising from her bodily promptings. Her brain is much smaller than that of the worker. In a dozen different ways she is inferior to the common worker-bees, who rule her absolutely, mapping out her entire daily life and using her for the good of the colony, just as a delicate costly piece of mechanism is used by human craftsmen to produce some necessary article.'

serves 4

1 lb [500 g] **parboiled potatoes**
4 medium tomatoes
1 green pepper, de-seeded
1 onion, sliced
1 dessertspoon [1×10 ml spoon] **flour**
4 oz [100 g] **Cheddar cheese, grated**
¼ pint [125 ml] **milk**
fat for frying
salt and pepper

Lightly fry the onion, tomato and sliced pepper.
Mix the cheese with the flour, and reserve 1/3 as topping.
Layer the potatoes, vegetable mixture and cheese in a greased casserole. Season each layer.
Pour in the milk.
Sprinkle with the remaining cheese. Cover with lid or foil.
Bake in a hot oven 400°F (200°C), Gas Mark 6, for 45 minutes, removing cover 10 minutes before the end of cooking to allow cheese to brown.

Stuffed Marrow

serves 4

1 vegetable marrow
Stuffing:
8 oz [250 g] potato, mashed
1 oz [25 g] onion, finely chopped
8 oz [250 g] cooked minced beef
3 tomatoes, chopped
2 oz [50 g] butter, melted
1 teaspoon [1 × 5 ml spoon]
   savoury sauce
salt and pepper

Peel the marrow, slice off one
end. With a long bladed knife or
narrow spoon, scoop out the seed
portion.
Mix together the ingredients for
the stuffing and press into the
cavity through the centre of the
marrow.
Cover the dish with a lid or with
well greased paper and bake at
375°F (190°C), Gas Mark 5, for
50-60 minutes or until the marrow
is tender.
Serve with brown gravy.

The Board is very proud of its
Cookery Demonstration Service
which for many years has been
the envy of food organisations
throughout the country. In any
year over six hundred demonstra-
tions are given to women's groups
in England, Scotland and Wales
and such is the popularity of the
service that bookings often have
to be made up to two years in
advance.

As an extension to this service, the
Board organises a series of Potato
Evenings each Autumn. These
shows, which are held in towns
and cities all over the country,
attract audiences of between 400
and 1000 people and consist of an
entertaining two-hour programme
during which the audience is
given the opportunity to put
questions to a panel of potato
experts.

Country Vegetarian Pie

serves 4

1 lb [500 g] **potatoes, boiled**
4 oz [100 g] **mushrooms, wiped
    and sliced**
4 oz [100 g] **peas, cooked**
4 **hard boiled eggs, sliced**
¼ **pint** [125 ml] **milk**
4 oz [100 g] **Cheddar cheese,
    grated**
1 oz [25 g] **butter**
salt and pepper

Slice the potatoes ¼ inch (0.5 cm)
thick.
Cook the mushrooms in butter
until tender.
Grease a pie dish, and place the
potatoes, peas, mushrooms and
sliced eggs in layers, adding salt
and pepper to taste.
Add the milk, cover with grated
cheese and bake in a hot oven
400°F (200°C), Gas Mark 6 for
20-30 minutes.
Serve piping hot.

Golden Leaves

serves 4

1 lb [500 g] **potatoes, peeled**
2 **eggs**
fat for frying
salt and pepper

Grate the potato into a bowl and
pour off the excess water.
Add the salt, pepper and eggs and
mix thoroughly.
Place dessertspoons (10 ml
spoons) of the mixture in fat and
fry until golden brown for about
10 minutes, turning half way
through cooking.
Drain on kitchen paper.

Country Pie

serves 4

1 lb [500 g] **duchesse potatoes**
8 oz [250 g] **carrots**
8 oz [250 g] **celery**
8 oz [250 g] **cauliflower**
8 oz [250 g] **onions**
can condensed celery soup

Dice the celery and carrots, divide
the cauliflower into sprigs, and
slice the onions.
Boil the vegetables together in
salted water until tender.
Drain and place in a pie dish.
Cover with the tin of undiluted
condensed soup.
Pipe the duchesse potatoes over
the vegetables, covering the top
completely.
Bake in a hot oven 400°F
(200°C), Gas Mark 6, for 30
minutes until top is nicely
browned.

Lemon Potatoes

serves 4

1 lb [500 g] **potatoes, sieved or
    riced**
1 oz [25 g] **butter**
1 **egg**
rind of 1 lemon
a pinch of thyme
salt and pepper

Add the butter, egg, rind and
thyme to the potatoes, beating
until smooth. Season.
Fill a piping bag, fitted with a star
nozzle, with potatoes.
Pipe rosettes on to a greased
baking sheet and bake at 400°F
(200°C), Gas Mark 6, till golden
brown.

New Potatoes and Cucumber with Cream

serves 4

1 lb [500 g] **new potatoes**
½ **cucumber**
3 **tablespoons** [3×20 ml spoons]
   single cream
freshly ground black pepper
salt

Scrub or scrape the potatoes.
Cook in boiling salted water.
Peel the cucumber and cut into 3,
then cut lengthwise into batons of
about ½ inch (1 cm) long.
Place in pan of boiling salted
water and simmer for 3-4
minutes. Drain.
Heat the cream, without boiling,
in a saucepan.
Add the potatoes and cucumber
and toss in the cream.
Serve with black pepper.

Batter Potatoes

serves 4

1 lb [500 g] **potatoes, parboiled**
   for 10 minutes
4 oz [100 g] **flour**
1 **egg**
¼ **pint** [125 ml] **milk**
a pinch of mixed herbs
fat for frying
salt and pepper

Prepare the batter by gradually
beating in the egg and milk to the
flour, herbs, salt, until smooth.
Cut the potatoes lengthwise, into
slices ¼ inch (0.5 cm) thick.
Dip each slice into the batter and
deep fry until golden and crisp.

Soufflé Baked Potatoes

serves 4

4 **large potatoes, scrubbed**
2 **eggs**
2 oz [50 g] **butter**
salt and pepper

Prick the potatoes with a fork and
brush with melted butter.
Bake in a hot oven 425°F
(220°C), Gas Mark 7, until soft.
Cut the potatoes in half
lengthwise and scoop out the
pulp.
Separate the egg yolks from the
whites and beat the yolks, butter
and seasoning into the potato
pulp, then fold in the stiffly
whisked egg white.
Place the mixture into the shells
and return to the oven for
10 minutes to reheat.

Boston Roast Potatoes

serves 4

1 lb [500 g] **potatoes, peeled**
   and parboiled
salt

After simmering the potatoes for
about 5 minutes, drain, and when
cool enough to handle, score the
surface of the potatoes with the
prongs of a fork.
Dip in melted fat and place
around the roast for about 1-1¼
hours at 425°F (220°C), Gas
Mark 7, basting occasionally.
To serve, sprinkle with a little
salt.

The Potato

It is to the Spaniards that we owe
this valuable esculent. The
Spaniards met with it in the
neighbourhood of Quito, where it
is cultivated by the natives. In
Spanish books published around
1553 the potato is mentioned
under the name 'battata' or
'papa'. Professor Edward Morren
states that the potato was introduced into England by John
Hawkins in 1563. If this be so, it
is a question whether the English
and not the Spaniards are not
entitled to the credit for the first
introduction; but according to Sir
Joseph Banks, the plant brought
by Drake and Hawkins was not
the common English potato but
the sweet potato.

In 1585 or 1586 potato tubers
were brought from North Carolina
to Ireland on the return of the
colonists sent out by Sir Walter
Raleigh, and were first cultivated
on Sir Walter Raleigh's estate
near Cork.

The Encyclopaedia Brittanica
1911

Fish and Potato Supper

Roast Potatoes

1 lb (500g) potatoes, peeled and of even size
oil
Salt and pepper

Pour sufficient oil in the roast pan to cover the base. Add the potatoes and season with salt and pepper. Baste with the oil. Place in the oven 220°C (425°F), Gas Mark 7, for 1 – 1½ hours. Turn several times during cooking to ensure even browning.

serves 4

1½ **lb [750 g] new potatoes, boiled**
8 oz [250 g] **smoked haddock, cooked**
½ **teaspoon [2.5 ml] made mustard**
1 **teaspoon [1×5 ml spoon] curry powder**
a few drops Worcestershire sauce
2 **tablespoons [2×20 ml spoons] milk**
¾ **pint [375 ml] milk**
1½ **oz [37 g] butter**
1½ **oz [37 g] flour or cornflour**
2 **oz [50 g] green peas or mushrooms, cooked**
salt and pepper

Drain and flake the fish, and mix it with the mustard, curry powder, sauce and two tablespoons (2×20 ml spoons) milk.
Place it in an ovenproof dish.
Slice the cooked potatoes and place them on top.
Make a white sauce with the milk, butter and flour, cooking it until it is smooth and thickens. Season to taste.
Pour over the contents of the dish to coat and cover the potatoes.
Bake in a moderate oven 350°F (180°C), Gas Mark 4, for about 20 minutes until thoroughly heated.
When the dish is nearly ready, sprinkle peas or chopped mushrooms on top.
Heat through, then serve.

Scalloway Flan   Sea Food Hotpot

He is probably the most famous character in the district and certainly the most sought after. He lives in a pool below the willow past the bridge and here he gives audience. Never a crowd, for one of the unwritten laws among fishermen transforms what in these circumstances would be a common queue, into a series of tactful visits, one at a time. There's nothing so restful as watching fish and so I found myself constantly being drawn to that willow past the bridge. More often than not I left my rod behind and took with me instead some of my problems, and as I watched the sleek manoeuvring of the fish below me, his swift decisive action or just his quiet toeing-the-line in mid-stream, my mind would clear itself of a number of things. He even cured me of his own slightly hypnotic effect on me; for one evening as I sat in my usual spot on the bank, my mind filled with a variety of ifs and buts, I consciously found myself watching for symbols. If he darts to the left it means this . . . if he darts to the right it means that . . . if he dashes downstream it must be this . . . and so on.

Suddenly, as my concentration intensified, a piece of thistledown floated out of the dusk on the water just in front of his nose, he leapt.

The huge flash left an ever-widening circle of ripples on the surface. And when they cleared I saw the thistledown floating past him downstream.

'All that fuss over a bit of fluff,' I said out loud, in his direction, and for the first time for many days, I giggled.

Barbara Hargreaves

serves 4

1 lb [500 g] **potato, mashed**
2 tablespoons [2×20 ml spoons]
 flour
1×7 oz pkt frozen prawns
½ pint [250 ml] **white sauce**
2 hard boiled eggs, sliced
Parmesan cheese
salt and pepper
parsley, chopped

Blend together the potatoes and flour.
Shape into an 8 inch (20 cm) flan tin or shallow plate.
Bake at 400°F (200°C), Gas Mark 6, for 10 minutes.
Prepare the filling, mixing together the sauce and prawns. Season.
Line the flan case with sliced eggs, reserving a few for decoration.
Reheat the sauce, pour into the flan and sprinkle liberally with the Parmesan cheese.
Cook for a further 20 minutes at 375°F (190°C), Gas Mark 5.
Garnish with sliced egg and chopped parsley.

serves 4

1 lb [500 g] **new potatoes**
1 lb [500 g] **filleted cod**
3 oz [75 g] **butter**
2 onions, finely chopped
nutmeg
4 oz [100 g] **shrimps**
3 oz [75 g] **mushrooms, sliced**
4 tablespoons [4×20 ml spoons]
 dry cider or white wine
lemon twists
parsley
salt and pepper

Cut the fish into four neat portions and fry until golden in a little butter.
Scrape the potatoes and slice wafer thin and place half in the base of the casserole. Sprinkle with nutmeg.
Fry the onions in 1 oz (25 g) of the butter and add to casserole.
Place the fish over the onions, follow with shrimps, mushrooms and liquid. Top with the remaining potatoes.
Brush over with the remaining butter and cook for one hour at 350°F (180°C), Gas Mark 4.
Decorate with lemon twists and parsley.

Fish Balls with Lemon

serves 4

1½ lb [750 g] **potatoes, sieved or riced**
1 lb [500 g] **smoked haddock**
2 tablespoons [2×20 ml spoons] **milk**
1 **bay leaf**
2 **eggs, hard boiled and finely chopped**
beaten egg to bind
1 **lemon**
1 tablespoon [1×20 ml spoon] **parsley, chopped**
fat for frying
salt and pepper

Simmer the fish in milk with the bay leaf, and when cooked remove the skin and bones and then flake.
Mix together the fish, potato and hard boiled eggs with sufficient beaten egg to bind.
Shape into balls and fry in butter or oil for 6-8 minutes turning frequently till they are golden brown.
Garnish with lemon wedges.

Findhorn Pie

serves 4

1 lb [500 g] **Duchesse potato**
8 oz [250 g] **smoked haddock**
4 oz [100 g] **bacon, crisply fried**
½ pint [250 ml] **milk**
1 dessertspoon [1×10 ml spoon] **cornflour**
1 oz [25 g] **butter**
salt and pepper

Cut the haddock into pieces and put in a saucepan with the butter and milk; bring to the boil and simmer gently until the fish is cooked.
Add the chopped up, crisply fried bacon.
Mix the cornflour with a little milk and add to the pan, shaking the pan vigorously as you do so.
Turn the mixture into a pie dish and pipe the duchesse mixture on top.
Place in a hot oven and bake at 400°F (200°C), Gas Mark 6, for 20 minutes until the top is nicely browned.

Stuffed Trout with Lemon Sauce

Dogger Bank Pie

serves 4

4 trout, cleaned and dried
Stuffing:
1 lb [500 g] potato, mashed
8 oz [250 g] mushrooms, finely chopped
1 teaspoon [1×5 ml spoon] dried thyme
1 tablespoon [1×20 ml spoon] parsley, chopped
1½ oz [35 g] butter
1 tablespoon [1×20 ml spoon] lemon juice
4 tablespoons [4×20 ml spoons] double cream
salt and pepper
Sauce:
6 oz [150 g] lemon marmalade
1 dessertspoon [1×10 ml spoon] lemon juice
3 oz [75 g] grapes, de-pipped

Prepare the stuffing by melting the butter in a pan, add the mushrooms, and cook till tender.
Place in a bowl the potatoes, thyme, parsley, lemon juice, mushrooms, cream and salt and pepper. Mix well together.
Divide the mixture between the four trout, place on a greased baking sheet and cover with foil.
Place in the oven, 350°F (180°C), Gas Mark 4, and cook for 45 minutes.
Make the sauce by slowly dissolving the marmalade with the lemon juice, stirring gently.
Add the grapes and allow to warm in the sauce.
Place the trout on a serving dish and pour over the sauce, or if preferred, serve in a sauce boat.

serves 4

1½ lb [750 g] potatoes, parboiled for 10 minutes and sliced
1½ lb [750 g] cod, skinned
½ pint [250 ml] milk
1 bayleaf
1 dessertspoon [1×10 ml spoon] parsley
3 oz [75 g] butter
1 large leek, sliced to ¾ inch [2 cm] thick
4 oz [100 g] mushrooms, chopped
½ a lemon, juice only
1 teaspoon [1×5 ml spoon] paprika
1½ oz [35 g] flour
salt and pepper

Poach the fish in milk with the bayleaf, parsley, salt and pepper for 10 minutes. Remove the bones and flake. Retain the milk.
Melt 1½ oz (37 g) of the butter in a pan and cook the leeks and mushrooms till soft.
Prepare a white sauce by melting the remaining butter.
Add the flour and cook for a minute, then gradually add the fish liquor to make a thick sauce. Season with salt, pepper and paprika.
Place half of the potato slices in the base of a greased casserole, cover with layers of flaked fish, leek and mushrooms and sauce. Top with the remaining potato slices.
Brush with a little melted butter and cook at 375°F (190°C), Gas Mark 5, for 30 minutes till the potatoes are golden brown.

Tuna Stuffed Baked Potatoes

serves 4

4 ready baked potatoes
8 tablespoons [8×20 ml spoons]
** fresh sour cream**
7 oz [175 g] tuna steak
2 tablespoons [2×20 ml spoons]
** chives, chopped**
salt and pepper

Cut the potatoes in half
lengthwise.
Scoop out the potato, reserving
the skins.
Mix together the potato, tuna
steak, cream, chives, salt and
pepper and pile back into the
skins.
Reheat under the grill or in a hot
oven, 400°F (200°C), Gas
Mark 6.

Potato and Herring Savoury Salad

serves 4

6 potatoes, cooked and diced
1 stalk celery, chopped
1 herring, cooked and flaked
1 lettuce heart, shredded
outer lettuce leaves to garnish
1 tablespoon [1×20 ml spoon] oil
1 dessertspoon [1×10 ml spoon]
** vinegar**
salt and pepper

Mix together the oil, vinegar, salt
and pepper.
Place all the other ingredients into
a bowl and blend with the
dressing.
Pile the salad on to a dish and
surround with lettuce.
Chill before serving.

To secure a good haul, some
superstitious fishermen throw
back into the water the first fish
they catch. Provided, of course,
it's not that proverbial one that
gets away!

The Brigadier's Special

serves 4

1 lb [500 g] **potatoes, peeled and boiled**
4 oz [100 g] **cheese, grated**
3 eggs, separated
½ oz [12.5 g] **butter**
a little milk
a pinch of cayenne pepper
salt and pepper
Filling:
8 oz [250 g] **flaked cod or haddock**
4 oz [100 g] **mushrooms, cooked and sliced**
4 oz [100 g] **herring roes, cooked**
1 can lobster soup
1 lemon
salt and pepper

Sieve the potatoes and beat in egg yolks, cheese, butter and milk.
Season with salt, pepper and cayenne pepper.
Whisk the egg whites until stiff and fold very lightly into the mixture.
Pour into a greased ring mould or savarin ring.
Bake in a hot oven at 425°F (220°C), Gas Mark 6, for 30-40 minutes.
Prepare the filling by placing all the ingredients in a saucepan and reheat.
Turn out ring on to a hot serving dish, then pour the filling into the centre.
Garnish with lemon wedges or slices and fresh prawns.

Salmon Bakes

serves 4

4 **potatoes, baked in jackets**
2 oz [50 g] **butter**
8 oz [250 g] **salmon**
tartare sauce to moisten
salt and pepper

Cut the baked potatoes in half lengthwise.
With a spoon, scoop out the potato into a bowl, add butter, salt and pepper, and mash well.
Fold in the salmon and tartare sauce.
Replace the mixture in the potato shells and bake at 375°F (190°C), Gas Mark 5, for 15 minutes or heat under a gentle grill.

Pilchard Cakes

serves 4

1 lb [500 g] **potatoes, mashed**
8 oz can **pilchards in tomato sauce**
1 teaspoon [1×5 ml spoon] **anchovy essence (optional)**
1 egg, beaten
breadcrumbs to coat
oil
salt and pepper

Place the potatoes, pilchards and sauce in a bowl and blend thoroughly. Season.
Form into cakes of 2 inch (5 cm) diameter by ½ inch (1 cm) thick.
Coat in egg and breadcrumbs.
Fry in shallow fat till cakes are golden brown. Drain.

Salmon Soufflé

serves 4

1 cup **potatoes, sieved or riced**
1 cup **poached salmon, flaked**
2 tablespoons [2×20 ml spoons] **milk**
2 tablespoons [2×20 ml spoons] **lard**
2 eggs
lemon juice
1 teaspoon [1×5 ml spoons] **parsley, chopped**
salt and pepper

Place the lard and milk in a saucepan, bring to the boil, and add the potatoes. Beat until thoroughly heated.
Separate the eggs and add the yolks to the potatoes with the fish, parsley, salt, pepper, and squeeze of lemon juice.
Beat the egg whites till stiff, and fold lightly into the mixture.
Turn into a greased pie dish or mould and bake in a hot oven, 425°F (220°C), Gas Mark 7, till well risen and golden brown.
Garnish with parsley.

Herrings with Potato Stuffing

serves 4

4 good sized herrings
Potato Stuffing:
12 oz [375 g] **potato, cooked and
  sieved**
1 oz [25 g] **butter**
2 teaspoons [2×5 ml spoons]
  parsley, chopped
1 oz [25 g] **onion, chopped**
1 teaspoon [1×5 ml spoon] **made
  mustard**
a pinch of mixed herbs
1 egg, beaten
1 lemon
salt and pepper

Prepare the herrings by removing
heads and backbones and rub
away the black skin with cooking
salt.
Wash and dry the fish.
Stuffing:
Melt the butter.
Mix together all the ingredients,
using the melted butter. Make
sure the seasoning is sufficient to
taste.
Divide the stuffing between each
fish.
Either roll up the herrings, heads
to tails, or fold in half to normal
shape. Tie round with cotton to
secure, and bake in a greased
covered casserole at 400°F
(200°C), Gas Mark 6, for 20
minutes.
Serve garnished with lemon
butterflies.

437.—ROUGH CHERVIL.
CHÆROPHYLLUM TEMULUM. J. 1038.2.
White. Stem spotted. 3 ft. July.

HAUNT OF THE DRAGON-FLY.

Potato and Haddock Soufflé

serves 4

1 lb [500 g] **potatoes, peeled and boiled**
4-6 oz [100-150 g] **smoked haddock, finely flaked**
4 eggs
1 oz [25 g] **butter**
2 tablespoons [2×20 ml spoons] **cream**
a few thin slices cucumber
cayenne pepper
salt and pepper

Sieve the potatoes and blend with the fish, egg yolks, butter and cream.
Season with salt, pepper and cayenne.
Whisk the egg whites until stiff and fold lightly into the fish mixture.
Pour into a greased souffle dish and bake in a hot oven at 425°F (220°C), Gas Mark 7.
Garnish with twists of cucumber.

Sole Otero

serves 4

4 large potatoes, baked in jackets
1 egg
1 oz [25 g] **butter**
4 fillets of sole, rolled and poached
2 oz [50 g] **prawns**
2 oz [50 g] **mushrooms, cut in quarters and poached**
½ pint [250 ml] **Mornay sauce**
Cheddar cheese, grated

Bake the potatoes, and scoop out the inside. Mash, and add the beaten egg and butter.
Pipe a border round potato shells.
Put rolled fillets of sole inside shells. Add the prawns and mushrooms and coat with Mornay sauce.
Sprinkle the top with grated cheese and return to a hot oven 425°F (220°C), Gas Mark 7, to glaze the top and reheat the potatoes.

Shrimp Potato Bake

serves 4

1 lb [500 g] **new potatoes, scrubbed and boiled**
4 oz [100 g] **shelled shrimps**
2 hard boiled eggs, sliced
2 oz [50 g] **fresh breadcrumbs**
¼ pint [125 ml] **single cream**
1-2 oz [25-50 g] **butter**
salt and pepper

Slice the potatoes about ¼ inch (0.5 cm) thick and place in a greased pie dish.
Reserve a few shrimps for garnish.
Cover the potatoes with shrimps and season, hard boiled eggs and breadcrumbs.
Pour the cream over to top, dot with butter, and bake in oven at 400°F (200°C), Gas Mark 6 for 15-20 minutes.
Decorate with shrimps before serving.

Dr Johnson thought, 'It is very strange, and very melancholy, that the paucity of human pleasures should persuade us ever to call hunting one of them.' While Oscar Wilde summed it up as 'the unspeakable in full pursuit of the uneatable.' It was R.S. Surtees with his famous character Jorrocks, the sporting grocer, who exploited the humorous possibilities of the sport. ''Unting is the sport of kings, the image of war without its guilt, and only five-and-twenty per cent of its danger! In the word, ''unting,' wot a ramification of knowledge is compressed! the choice of an 'oss - the treatment of him when got - the groomin' at home, the ridin' abroad - the boots, the breeches, the saddle, the bridle, the 'ound, the 'untsman, the feeder, the Fox! Oh, how that beautiful word, Fox, gladdens my 'eart, and warms the declinin' embers of my age.'

Poacher's Tasties

Tomato Scallop

Curried Fish Favourite

serves 4

1 lb [500 g] **potatoes**
4 oz [100 g] **plain flour**
Filling:
7½ oz can pink salmon
2 dessertspoons [2×10 ml spoons]
    tartare sauce
fat for frying
salt and pepper

Blend together the potatoes and
flour.
Knead on a floured board and roll
out to ¼ inch (0.5 cm) thick.
Cut into rounds of about 4 inches
(10 cm). Damp the edges.
Flake the salmon, and add the
sauce, and salt and pepper to
taste.
Place some of the mixture along
the centre of the pastry, fold over
and knock up the edges and flute.
Place in deep fat and fry till
golden. Drain.
Can be eaten hot with vegetables
or cold with mixed salad.

serves 4

1 lb [500 g] **potatoes, creamed**
12 oz [375 g] **white fish**
2 tablespoons [2×20 ml spoons]
    milk
2 tablespoons [2×20 ml spoons]
    breadcrumbs, white
2 oz [50 g] **Cheddar cheese, grated**
can condensed tomato and rice
    soup
salt and pepper

Cut the fish into pieces and put
into a saucepan with the milk and
can of undiluted condensed soup.
Season and simmer until the fish
is cooked.
Pipe a border of creamed potato
round a shallow ovenproof dish
and fill the centre with the fish
mixture.
Mix the cheese and breadcrumbs
together and sprinkle on top.
Place under the grill until the
potatoes are browned and the
cheese is golden and bubbly.
Instead of one large dish, use four
scallop shells.

serves 4

1 lb [500 g] **potatoes, peeled and**
    boiled
1 lb [500 g] **cod or haddock**
1 oz [25 g] **butter**
1 onion, chopped
1 apple, peeled and grated
1 oz [25 g] **flour**
1 tablespoon [1×20 ml spoon]
    curry powder
1 oz [25 g] **raisins**
1 tablespoon [1×20 ml spoon]
    chutney
salt and pepper

Poach the fish in water for 10-15
minutes. Drain, and reserve the
liquid.
Slice the potatoes.
Make the sauce by melting the
butter and frying the onion and
apple; add the flour and curry
powder and mix well then add
½ pint liquid (250 ml).
Add the raisins, chutney, salt and
pepper.
Simmer gently while skinning and
boning the fish.
Place layers of fish and potato in
an ovenproof dish and pour over
the sauce.
Reheat in the oven at 375°F
(190°C), Gas Mark 5, for
20 minutes.

The Monumental Brass

The monumental brass to Sir Robert de Septvans was laid in 1306 in Chartham church, and remains, tucked in behind the modern organ, as one of the best and earliest we have. In full chain mail with decorated broad sword, wearing an elegant surcoat embroidered with the punning arms of his family - seven winnowing fans - chain mail hood thrown back to reveal his curly flowing hair, he gazes across the centuries.

Thousands of rubbings of this brass have been taken, and hundreds have gone all over the world to places undiscovered and undreamed of when Sir Robert was a famous knight.

Between 1300 and 1600 thousands of brasses were laid in our parish churches, cathedrals and abbeys, and many of them destroyed in turn by Henry VIII, Cromwell and the Victorians. Those that remain, the best in beautiful little parish churches where those vandals never found them, are a wonderful record of our people, our history, our costumes, and our heritage. To study them by rubbing them, photographing them, or just looking at them, is just about the most rewarding and peaceful hobby there is. One goes in looking for brasses and comes out with so much more.

Potato Tugs

serves 4

4 large potatoes, scrubbed
8 fillets of sole
2 oz [50 g] butter
8 slices of processed cheese
salt and pepper

Prick the potatoes using a fork, brush them with melted fat and bake in a hot oven 425°F (220°C), Gas Mark 7.

Roll up the fillets of sole and poach or bake them for 15 minutes.

When the potatoes are cooked, cut in half lengthwise, remove the pulp, beat in the butter and seasoning, then pile the mixture back into the shells.

Top each potato with one fillet of sole and cover with a cheese slice.

Grill or bake until the cheese melts and serve hot.

Watermills

The earliest fully mechanised way to grind corn, the first type of watermill was a roofed two-level bridge over a stream. On the top floor was a fixed 'bedstone' with a hole through the middle. A vertical shaft carrying the 'runner stone' just above the 'bedstone' passed down through it and the framework into the bed of the stream, with horizontal paddles attached to the bottom, turned by the flow of the water. The Romans invented the 'modern' watermill by setting the paddle-wheel vertically in the stream, the horizontal axle passing into a millhouse on the bank. A gear wheel on the inside end of this axle turned smaller gear wheels on vertical spindles which carried the runner stones in the grinding floor above.

Between 5000 and 6000 watermills of this type were recorded in the Domesday Book.

Water comes from a dam which holds enough water to turn the mill consistently. A sluice gate releases water onto the mill wheel. If it runs onto and under the bottom of the wheel it turns it anti-clockwise, and is known as 'undershot'. If the water falls on the side of the wheel it also turns anti-clockwise and is 'breastshot'. If it is led out over the top of the wheel to fall on the front of it and turn it clockwise, it is 'overshot'. To stop a watermill you just shut the sluice gate.

Water power is much more constant and controllable than wind power so in areas where water was plentiful, watermills were very common, and windmills rare. A tall weatherboarded watermill reflected in a calm millpond overhung with willow trees, under summer sunshine, has an air of tranquility entirely lacking in a working windmill.

68

Salmon and New Potato Pie

serves 4

1½ **lb** [750 g] **new potatoes, parboiled for 10 minutes**
7½ **oz can pink salmon, flaked**
2 **eggs**
¼ **pint** [125 ml] **single cream**
1 **tablespoon** [1 × 20 ml spoon] **onion, grated**
butter
1 **tablespoon** [1 × 20 ml spoon] **Worcestershire sauce**
salt and pepper

Cut the potatoes into slices and place half on the base of a greased casserole.
Beat the eggs with cream, sauce, salt and pepper.
Mix in the salmon and onion and place in the casserole.
Place the remaining potatoes on top and brush with melted butter.
Cook in a moderate oven at 350°F (180°C), Gas Mark 4, for 30 minutes.

Stuffed Baked Mackerel with Gooseberries

serves 4

8 oz [250 g] **potatoes, peeled and diced**
4 **mackerel, prepared**
1 **medium sized can of gooseberries**
2 tablespoons [2×20 ml spoons] **tartare sauce**
a **few sprigs of parsley**
2 **slices of tomato**
salt and pepper

Mix together the drained gooseberries, tartare sauce and potatoes.
Fill each mackerel with some of the potato mixture, wrap each fish in foil and place in an ovenproof dish.
Bake for 30-40 minutes at 350°F (180°C), Gas Mark 4, and when cooked unwrap and serve on an oval platter garnished with sliced tomatoes and sprigs of parsley.

Potato Kipper Scramble

serves 4

1 ¾ lb [875 g] **potatoes, boiled**
1-2 **kippers, grilled**
6 **eggs**
1 tablespoon [1×20 ml spoon] **cream, or top of milk**
salt and pepper

Bone the kippers and flake them. (Keep warm).
Beat the eggs, salt and pepper lightly together.
Scramble the eggs in a buttered pan (with the heat low and stirring all the time).
Remove from the heat, stir in the cream and most of the kippers.
Drain the potatoes, arrange in a ring, pile the eggs in the centre and decorate with the remaining kipper.
(Boil-in-the-bag kippers can be used).

Haddock Darioles

serves 4

1 lb [500 g] **potatoes, boiled**
1 lb [500 g] **smoked haddock, cooked**
1 oz [25 g] **butter**
1 **egg**
parsley, chopped
cayenne pepper
salt and pepper

Chop the fish finely.
Mash the potatoes with milk and butter, cayenne pepper, salt and pepper to taste, and egg yolk, and combine with fish.
Fold in the stiffly beaten egg white and chopped parsley.
Place the mixture in well greased Dariole moulds and bake in oven at 350°F (180°C), Gas Mark 4, for 15 minutes.
Serve immediately.

Izaak Walton's recipe for the Compleat Angler - 'he that hopes to be a good angler, must not only bring an inquiring, searching, observing wit, but he must bring a large measure of hope and patience, and a love and propensity to the art itself; but having once got and practised it, then doubt not but anything will prove to be so pleasant, that it will prove to be, like virtue, a reward to itself.'

Tarbert Salad

serves 4

1 lb [500 g] **new potatoes, cooked**
4 oz [100 g] **prawns**
6 tablespoons [6×20 ml spoons]
   mayonnaise
2 tablespoons [2×20 ml spoons]
   tomato ketchup
1 teaspoon [1×5 ml spoon]
   Worcestershire sauce
parsley, freshly chopped
lettuce and cucumber
juice of ¼ of a lemon
salt and pepper

Mix together the mayonnaise,
ketchup, Worcestershire sauce
and lemon juice.
Cut the potatoes into dice and add
the prawns.
Blend with the dressing.
Serve on a bed of lettuce
garnished with parsley and
cucumber.

Tuna Savoury

serves 4

1 lb [500 g] **Duchesse potato**
Filling:
7½ [175 g] **tuna steak, flaked**
8 oz **can tomatoes, peeled**
a pinch of chilli powder
4 **eggs, beaten**
4 tablespoons [4×20 ml spoons]
   double cream
salt

Pipe the potatoes on the base and
around the edge of a greased
ovenproof dish.
Blend together the tuna steak,
tomatoes, chilli powder, and salt.
Add the cream to the eggs and
mix in with the other ingredients.
Place into the potato shell and
bake in a moderate oven, 350°F
(180°C), Gas Mark 4, for 30-35
minutes until the egg is set.

Potato Temptation

serves 4

2 lb [1 kg] **potatoes, thinly sliced**
1 **can anchovy fillets in oil**
2 **large onions, in thin rings**
4 oz [100 g] **button mushrooms**
   thinly sliced
2½ oz [62 g] **butter**
7½ fl oz [175 ml] **cream**
pepper

Arrange half the potatoes in a well
buttered casserole.
Melt half the butter in a pan, add
the mushrooms, and cook gently
for 3 minutes.
Cover the potatoes in the dish
with the onions, mushrooms and
anchovies, reserving the oil and
place the remaining potatoes on
top.
Pour over half the cream and oil
from the can; dot with the
remaining butter and bake at
400°F (200°C), Gas Mark 6, for
45 minutes.
Pour over the remaining cream,
and cook for a further 10 minutes.

A Memory

Four ducks on a pond,
   A grass-bank beyond,
A blue sky of spring,
   White clouds on the wing;
What a little thing
   To remember for years -
To remember with tears!

Lemon Rabbit

The Hedger

serves 4

Topping:
1½ lb [750 g] potatoes, sieved or riced
½ oz [12.5 g] butter
1 egg
a pinch of dried mixed herbs
rind of 1 lemon
salt and pepper
Filling:
1 lb [500 g] rabbit meat, cooked
Sauce:
½ oz [12.5 g] butter
½ oz [12.5 g] flour
¼ pint [125 ml] white stock
¼ pint [125 ml] fresh sour cream
salt and pepper

Place all the ingredients for the topping into a bowl and beat thoroughly.
Melt the butter in a pan, add the flour and cook for a minute without browning.
Add the white stock gradually, stirring continuously until smooth.
Add the sour cream, salt and pepper. Allow to heat but do not boil.
Mix the sauce with the rabbit and place in a greased casserole.
Place potato into a piping bag fitted with a star nozzle and cover the filling.
Place in oven and cook at 375°F (190°C), Gas Mark 5, for 30 minutes.

How much longer we shall see hand-laid hedges depends on how many young men learn a craft which is no longer passed on from father to son. Unfortunately mechanical trimmers work out cheaper. Yet still hedgers turn up for National Championships, for sheep fencing from the Welsh borders and cattle fencing from the Midlands. Each man has a heavy axe, a wooden rake, spade and mattock for digging out the 'weeds', a mallet, a slasher or hedge knife, and most important, a billhook. A descendant of the halberd or battle axe, this is a short handled tool, sometimes double edged, of which there are about forty regional patterns.

He sizes up the hedge and then cuts out unwanted wood and weeds. Then he partially severs the branches, low down so that they will bend without breaking or puckering the bark, and lays them to form a neat stockproof barrier. This barrier is held in place by upright stakes at about one yard intervals, and 'edders' or strips of pliable willow or hazel are woven in to make a neat top edge. When the new shoots grow up the hedge will form an impenetrable barrier. Each hedger works according to regional styles and these are tailored to the stock to be contained. Thus sheep fences must have no gaps at all. Where shelter is needed tall regrowth is encouraged. Even if not economically justified, it is to be hoped that craft and craftsman will never become obsolete.

Turkey Braise

Barbecued Game Flan

serves 4

1 lb [500 g] **potatoes, thinly sliced**
4 **turkey portions**
1 oz [25 g] **butter**
8 oz [250 g] **sliced onion or
    button onions**
1 oz [25 g] **butter**
1 **dessertspoon** [1×10 ml spoon]
    soft brown sugar
¼ **pint** [125 ml] **red wine**
¼ **pint** [125 ml] **white stock**
parsley
salt and pepper

Fry the turkey portions in butter
till golden brown and place in a
deep casserole.
Toss the onions in the butter and
sugar and place in the casserole
with the wine and stock. Season.
Place the potatoes in overlapping
slices on top and brush with a
little melted butter.
Cover and cook at 350°F (180°C),
Gas Mark 4, for 1¼ hours.
Remove the lid and cook for a
further 20 minutes at 400°F
(200°C), Gas Mark 6.

serves 4

2 lb [1 kg] **potatoes, mashed**
1 **egg**+half an egg
1 oz [25 g] **butter**
Filling:
1 lb [500 g] **cooked game:
    pheasant, partridge or grouse**
Sauce:
½ oz [12.5 g] **butter**
½ oz [12.5 g] **flour**
1 **small onion, finely chopped**
½ **pint** [250 ml] **white wine**
1 **level teaspoon** [1×5 ml spoon]
    crushed rosemary
2 **level teaspoons** [2×5 ml spoons]
    paprika pepper
2 **teaspoons** [2×5 ml spoons]
    Worcestershire sauce
salt and pepper
watercress

Grease a 7 inch (18 cm) flan case
or loose bottomed cake tin.
Add the beaten egg and butter to
the potatoes.
Line the tin with the potatoes,
bringing it up the sides, and
brush inside with a little beaten
egg.
Place in a hot oven and bake at
400°F (200°C), Gas Mark 6, for
about 30 minutes, until lightly
browned.
Remove carefully from the tin and
place on an ovenproof serving
dish. Keep warm.
Sauce:
Melt the butter in a pan, add the
onion and cook gently without
browning.
Add the flour and cook for a few
minutes.
Add the wine gradually, stirring
constantly, and then add the
Worcestershire sauce and paprika
pepper and game. Check
seasoning.
Pour into flan and garnish with
watercress.

72

Fricassée of Rabbit

serves 4

1 ¾ lb [875 g] **Duchesse potato**
1 young **rabbit, jointed**
½ **pint** [250 ml] **stock**
½ **pint** [250 ml] **milk**
4 oz [100 g] **streaky bacon,
  chopped**
4 **cloves**
1 large **onion**
1 blade **mace**
a pinch of **mixed herbs**
2 oz [50 g] **mushrooms, chopped**
1 oz [25 g] **butter**
1 oz [25 g] **flour**
parsley
salt and pepper

Place the rabbit joints into a
saucepan, add the stock, milk,
bacon, mace, herbs, mushrooms
and cloves which have been
pressed into the onion.
Bring to the boil and skim if
necessary.
Simmer gently for 1½-2 hours till
the rabbit is tender.
Place the rabbit in an ovenproof
dish and keep hot, reserving the
liquor for the sauce.
Pipe the duchesse potato around
the edge of the dish.
Melt the butter in a pan, stir in
the flour and cook without
browning.
Add the liquor gradually, stirring
constantly, until the sauce boils
and thickens.
Place over the rabbit joints.

Chicken Potato Pie

serves 4

4 oz [100 g] **potato, mashed**
1 **egg**
2 tablespoons [2 × 20 ml spoons]
  melted butter
1½ teaspoons [1½ × 5 ml spoons]
  baking powder
approx. 4 oz [100 g] **flour**
salt and pepper
Filling:
4 oz [100 g] **potatoes, cooked and
  diced**
8 oz [250 g] **chicken, cooked and
  diced**
4 oz [100 g] **peas, cooked**
4 oz [100 g] **carrots, cooked and
  diced**
½ **pint** [250 ml] **white sauce**
1 oz [25 g] **flour**
1 oz [25 g] **butter**
½ **pint** [250 ml] **milk**
2 tablespoons [2 × 20 ml spoons]
  sherry
salt and pepper

Blend together the potato, egg,
butter, salt and pepper.
Sift together the baking powder
and flour.
Add to the potato and mix well
together.
Set aside whilst preparing the
filling.

Filling:
Mix all the ingredients together.
Place in a greased pie dish.
Roll out the pastry to size and
cover the filling.
Bake in a hot oven, 400°F
(200°C), Gas Mark 6, for 20
minutes.

The Seasons

Spring in England begins in
March when the sun feels un-
expectedly warm out of the wind,
and greenness grows up into the
grass and is a haze in the willow
trees. Spring is March hares
leaping around the fields, regard-
less of hail and icy rain slashing
out of towering squalls in hard
blue skies. In spite of cold east
winds, encouraged by the sunshine, rooks nest in high bare
trees, lapwings tumble in court-
ship flights, and cuckoos call
unseen.

Summer begins in June when
the sun becomes warm enough for
hay-making or sunbathing. The
skies soften, and with luck the
wind goes southerly, and long fine
days encourage the roses to
bloom. By midsummer high
pressure weather brings long hot
spells under brassy skies, light
early morning dew and dry heat
which crackles the hay. Lower
pressure turns the wind westerly
and wide rain fronts sweep the
countryside. In late summer south
or northwest winds may bring big
storms in the afternoon or night,
and hot spells become shorter as
autumn takes over. Heavy dews
lead to early morning mists, and
later to more persistent mist and
fog. Usually there is plenty of rain
to restore the balance of a dry
summer. Berries ripen red, but it
takes the gales which come in
October to strip most of the
leaves. Autumn is wet, wild and
windy, but not particularly cold.

Dull November is the beginning
of winter, December may be
frosty, but January and February
are our coldest months. The bitter
north-easterly winds have to be
experienced to be believed. If it
snows, and we do sometimes have
prolonged spells, it will be the
grey cold of northern latitudes,
and cold wet weather can persist
well into March until 'all suddenly
the wind comes soft, and spring is
here again'.

Fig. 84.—Points of a Fowl.

REFERENCES.

1. Comb.
2. Face.
3. Wattles.
4. Deaf-ear or Ear-lobe.
5. Hackle.
6. Breast.
7. Back.
8. Saddle.
9. Saddle-hackles.

10. Sickles.
11. Tail-coverts.
12. True Tail-feathers.
13. Wing-bow.
14. Wing-coverts, forming the "bar."
15. Secondaries, the lower-ends forming the wing or lower butts. Wing-bay. Diamond.

16. Lower wing butts.
17. Primaries. Hidden by Secondaries when the wing is closed.
18. Thighs.
19. Hocks.
20. Legs or Shanks.
21. Spur.
22. Toes or Claws.

Chicken Pot Roast

serves 4

2 lb [1 kg] **small new potatoes,
  scrubbed**
2½-3 lb [1.5 kg] **boiling fowl,
  jointed**
4 oz [100 g] **bacon rashers**
1 large **carrot, diced**
1 small **turnip, diced**
4 oz [100 g] **peas**
4 oz [100 g] **mushrooms**
1 teaspoon [1×5 ml spoon] **mixed
  herbs**
white stock
clove of garlic
salt and pepper

Choose a heavy based pan or
ovenproof casserole and line the
base with the rashers of bacon.
Place in the chicken joints,
packing them tightly together.
Add in layers the vegetables,
finishing with the small new
potatoes on top and season with
salt and pepper.
Add sufficient stock to cover half
way up the pan.
Sprinkle with herbs.
Rub the inside of the lid with the
clove of garlic and place on the
pan, making sure it is fitting
closely.
Cook very slowly on top of the
cooker for 3 hours, or if in a
casserole, place in the oven at
300°F (150°C), Gas Mark 2, for
2½-3 hours.

Anglo-Saxon Chicken

serves 4

4 individual **chicken portions**
1 lb [500 g] **Duchesse potato**
1 oz [25 g] **butter**
2 tablespoons [2×20 ml spoons]
  cream
3 tablespoons [3×20 ml spoons]
  seasoned flour
1 **onion, large, sliced**
2 cloves **garlic**
¼ pint [125 ml] **beer**
1 **chicken stock cube**
salt and pepper

Dip the chicken joints in the
seasoned flour and fry in the
butter.
Add the sliced onion and the
crushed garlic and continue
frying.
Dissolve the stock cube in the beer
and add to the frying pan. Cover,
and allow to simmer for 30
minutes.
Pipe the duchesse potatoes in a
ring round a shallow dish, and
flash in a hot oven or under the
grill to brown.
Transfer the chicken joints to the
centre of the dish.
If the gravy left in the pan looks a
little thin, thicken with a teaspoon
(1×5 ml spoon) of cornflour and
then stir in the cream.
Pour the creamy gravy over the
chicken joints and serve
immediately.

The British Elm

Three main species of elm grow in
England. The Wych Elm 'ulmus
glabra', English Elm, 'ulmus
procera' and Smooth Leaved Elm,
'ulmus minor'. The Smooth
Leaved elm was introduced into
Britain in the Bronze age. The
Romans used elm extensively as a
forage plant, and for timber, and
it has always been planted as a
hedgerow shelter tree in rural
Britain. The English elm is
mainly a Midland species as is the
less plentiful Wych elm. The great
Smooth Leaved elms are a pre-
dominant feature of our countryside particularly in East Anglia.
The trees in those magnificent
Constable paintings of Suffolk are
Smooth Leaved elms.

There were epidemics of Dutch
elm disease (a fungus carried by
the 'Scolytus' beetle) in 1927 and
the 1930s, but they died down and
became endemic at a low level.
Since 1972 we have a terrible
epidemic and millions of trees are
dead or dying. In 1971 1.3 million
- one sixth of the total 8.7 million
elms were affected. At that rate
they will soon disappear al-
together. The worst hit areas are
near our ports, the Thames, the
Severn and Portsmouth areas, so
it seems as if the new strain of
fungus has been imported in
timber, with another live beetle
carrier. No known method, not
even felling and burning halts the
disease for more than a very short
time. In a back-handed way, the
trouble has stimulated the closer
study of trees which may help to
protect other species from similar
threats, such as oak wilt or
chestnut blight even if it is too late
to save the elm, which will take
several hundred years to regene-
rate from the few survivors, unless
a lot of replanting is done.

Sauté Potatoes and Chicken Livers

serves 4

2 lb [1 kg] **new potatoes, cooked and sliced**
1 lb [500 g] **chicken livers**
flour
garlic, crushed (optional)
parsley, chopped
salt and pepper

Sauté the potatoes in butter until crisp and golden brown.
Remove and keep warm.
Dip the chicken livers in seasoned flour and fry in a pan with the garlic.
Serve by arranging the chicken livers in the centre of an oval dish surrounded by crisp sauté potatoes.
Sprinkle liberally with chopped parsley.

That fine Wiltshire writer, Richard Jefferies, was rash enough to state, 'It takes a hundred and fifty years to make a beauty - a hundred and fifty years out-of-doors. Open air, hard manual labour or continuous exercise, good food, good clothing, some degree of comfort, all of these, but most especially open air, must play their part for five generations before a beautiful woman can appear. These conditions can only be found in the country, and consequently all beautiful women come from the country. Though the accident of birth may cause their register to be signed in town, they are always of country extraction.'

Duck Casserole

serves 4

1 lb [500 g] **potatoes, peeled and thinly sliced**
4 **portions of duck**
1 **medium sized onion**
3 **rashers bacon**
1 oz [25 g] **butter**
1 oz [25 g] **flour**
¼ **pint** [125 ml] **water**
a pinch of mixed herbs
chopped parsley and lemon wedges
salt and pepper

Wash and dry the duck portions and cut away any excess fat. Place in a large casserole.
Chop the onion and bacon and fry in butter till lightly browned. Stir in the flour and cook for a few minutes.
Add the water gradually and stir till the mixture boils and thickens.
Season with salt and pepper and add the herbs.
Pour the sauce over the duck.
Place the potatoes on top in a thick layer.
Brush with melted butter or fat and cover with a lid or foil.
Cook in a moderate oven, 350°F (180°C), Gas Mark 4, for 1½-2 hours.
Remove the lid for the last 30 minutes to allow the potatoes to brown.

Stuffed Roast Chicken

serves 4

1 **roasting chicken, oven ready about 4 lb** [2 kg]
1 **onion, grated**
1 **dessertspoon** [1 × 10 ml spoon] **pepper**
8 oz [250 g] **natural yoghurt**
Stuffing:
1 lb [500 g] **potatoes, cooked and riced**
1 **lemon, juice only**
2 **eggs, hardboiled and chopped**
2 **tablespoons** [2 × 20 ml spoons] **almonds, finely chopped**
4 oz [100 g] **raisins**
4 oz [100 g] **butter**
salt and pepper

Blend together the yoghurt, onion and pepper and pour over the chicken. Pierce the flesh with a fork or skewer to allow the marinade to penetrate the flesh. Set aside for about 2 hours.
Sprinkle the potatoes with the lemon juice, add the eggs and almonds.
Cover the raisins with boiling water for about 10 minutes to allow them to 'plump out'.
Drain and add to the potato mixture.
Place the stuffing in the neck and body of the chicken and secure the flesh with a wooden cocktail stick.
Melt the butter in a pan or ovenproof casserole and brown the chicken on all sides.
Cover with a lid or foil and cook in the oven at 375°F (190°C), Gas Mark 5 till tender - approx. 1½-2 hours.

Casserole of Hare with Potato Dumplings

serves 4

1½ lbs [750 g] **potatoes, peeled and quartered**
1 **hare, cut into joints**
2 **onions, finely chopped**
4 oz [100 g] **streaky bacon, diced**
2 **cloves garlic** (optional)
1 **glass red wine**
½ pint [250 ml] **stock**
1 tablespoon [1 × 20 ml spoon] **tomato purée**
salt and pepper

Fry the bacon over a gentle heat to allow the fat to run, remove from the pan.
Slightly brown the hare in the bacon fat and remove to a deep casserole.
Place wine, stock and tomato purée in a pan and bring to the boil, and let reduce a little.
Place potatoes, bacon, onion and garlic over the joints, and season.
Pour liquid into the casserole, cover with a tight fitting lid and cook very slowly in oven 300°F (150°C), Gas Mark 2, for 2-3 hours, until the hare is quite tender.

Dumplings:
8 oz [250 g] **potatoes, sieved or riced, cold**
3 oz [75 g] **self raising flour**
½ **an egg, beaten**
½ teaspoon [2.5 ml] **mixed herbs**

Work all the ingredients together vigorously to obtain a smooth firm dough.
Shape into dumplings about the size of a golf ball.
Drop into rapidly boiling salted water and remove when risen to the top.

THE HARE.

Potato Chick-Nut

serves 4

1½ lb [750 g] **potatoes, peeled and thinly sliced**
4 **chicken joints**
1½ oz [35 g] **butter**
small onion, chopped
1 **large stick celery, diced**
½ teaspoon [2.5 ml] **mixed herbs**
¾ oz [20 g] **plain flour**
3 oz [75 g] **crunchy peanut butter**
¾ pint [375 ml] **milk**
salt and pepper

Melt the butter in a pan.
Remove the skins from the chicken joints and fry on both sides for about 5 minutes.
Place some of the potato slices in a greased casserole, reserving the remainder for the top.
Place the chicken joints over the potatoes, add the onion and celery to the pan and fry for 5 minutes.
Add the flour and the herbs and seasoning and cook for a further 2-3 minutes.
Stir in the peanut butter and remove from the heat.
Add the milk gradually. Return to a low heat and stir until thickened. Pour over the chicken joints.
Place the remaining potato slices around the side of the dish and brush with a little melted butter.
Bake in the oven at 350°F (180°C), Gas Mark 4, for 1½ hours.

Turkey Pasties

Rabbit Roast

Chicken and Mushroom Pie

serves 4

1 lb [500 g] **potatoes, sieved or riced**
4 oz [100 g] **self raising flour**
8 oz [250 g] **cooked turkey, shredded**
¼ **pint** [125 ml] **bread sauce**
½ **teaspoon** [2.5 ml] **powdered cloves**
salt and pepper

Work the potatoes and flour together to form a smooth dough.
Roll out on a floured board to about ¼ inch (0.5 cm) thick and cut into rounds of about 5 inch (12.5 cm) diameter.
Add the powdered cloves and salt and pepper to the sauce and fold in the turkey.
Place the mixture along the centre of each round to within ½ inch (1 cm) of the edge.
Dampen edges, fold over and seal. Knock up the edges and flute with fingers. Place on a greased baking sheet and bake at 400°F (200°C), Gas Mark 6, for 20 minutes, until golden brown. Serve hot with vegetables.

Spread goosefat all over an old sock and wrap it round your neck on going to bed. By morning your sore throat will be gone. Your pillowslip (and hair) will be covered in grease, as will your nightclothes and the top sheet, but that is beside the point.

If cuts won't stop bleeding, gather a handful of cobwebs with your fingers and spread them on the wound. Make sure the cobwebs are not too dusty or infection of the wound may follow! There is probably a clotting agent in a cobweb or the belief would not be so widespread.

78

serves 4

1½ lb [750 g] **potatoes**
4 **rabbit joints**
1 **medium onion**
4 **rashers bacon**
1 **tablespoon** [1×20 ml spoon] **apple or redcurrant jelly**
about 2½ **fl oz** [65 ml] **stock or water**
1 **fl oz** [25 ml] **oil**
2 **level tablespoons** [2×20 ml spoons] **seasoned flour**
6 **peppercorns**
salt and pepper

Place the rabbit in cold water, bring to the boil and discard the water.
Coat the rabbit in seasoned flour and lay in the hot oil in a casserole.
Peel the potatoes and slice the onion, and place them round the meat in the dish.
Cover the rabbit with the bacon rashers.
Mix the redcurrant jelly with the stock, pour into the dish, and add the peppercorns.
Cover the dish and bake at 400°F (200°C), Gas Mark 6, for 1¼-1½ hours.

serves 4

1 lb [500 g] **Duchesse potato**
1 oz [25 g] **butter**
1 oz [25 g] **flour**
½ **pint** [250 ml] **milk**
1 lb [500 g] **chicken, cooked**
4 oz [100 g] **mushrooms, sliced and cooked**

Place the cooked chicken and mushrooms in a greased casserole.
Prepare the sauce by melting the butter in a pan, stirring in the flour, and cooking for 4 minutes, then gradually add the milk.
Pour the sauce over the chicken.
Spread or pipe the potato over the mixture and bake in an oven until browned, 400°F (200°C), Gas Mark 6, for 20-30 minutes.

Beef Soufflé

The Millwright

Nowadays there are less than a dozen millwrights in this country, engaged on freelance restoration work. The county of Essex actually employs a full time millwright, a young man who started his working life as a bank clerk and is now a fine craftsman. Too much restoration has been done in the past with the best intentions by builders without specialised knowledge, but only the man who knows his windmills inside out can do a perfect job.

He must be able to make and mend not only the structure and the sails with their complicated shuttering, but also the interior gearing and machinery. He must be builder, carpenter, smith, engineer, craftsman and perfectionist with a good head for heights.

In the days of cheap labour he had many helpers, but now he must work alone for much of the time. But there can be no greater satisfaction than, when after months of painstaking work, he can start the sails, and listen to the swish and clatter and rumble as a long-dead windmill moves slowly back into life.

serves 4

Topping:
1 lb [500 g] **potatoes, cooked, sieved or riced**
1 oz [25 g] **butter**
3 tablespoons [3×20 ml spoons] **cream**
2 oz [50 g] **Cheddar cheese, grated**
2 egg whites
Filling:
1 lb [500 g] **steak mince**
2 onions, finely chopped
2 oz [50 g] **butter**
2 tablespoons [2×20 ml spoons] **oil**
4 oz [100 g] **mushrooms, sliced**
½ pint [250 ml] **beef stock**
2 egg yolks
2 tablespoons [2×20 ml spoons] **tomato ketchup**
salt and pepper

Fry the onions in butter and oil for 3 minutes, then add the mince and cook till browned.
Add the mushrooms and stock, and season with salt and pepper.
Simmer for 45 minutes.
Remove from the heat, add the ketchup and beaten egg yolks, and place in a buttered soufflé dish.
Mix well together the potatoes, butter, cream and cheese.
Beat the egg whites till stiff and fold into the potato.
Place over the meat and cook at 400°F (200°C), Gas Mark 6, till golden brown - about 25-30 minutes.

The Thatcher

One country craftsman who is in great demand is the thatcher. For a time it seemed that thatched roofs would become a thing of the past; combine harvesters made the thatched corn stacks obsolete, and fewer thatchers passed on their trade to their sons. Now the trend has reversed, and the thatcher is never out of work. It is a pleasant job, done when the weather is reasonably fine, using natural materials and simple tools; combed wheat or rye straw (another rarity in these days of combines) or Norfolk reed. Norfolk reed is the most popular, having a life of up to 60 years. This is pegged down with hazel 'spars' over long strips or 'sways' of split hazel.

Thatchers often leave something in the roof for the next man to find. In the roof of a Kent cottage a thatcher found an obsolete thatching tool and an old mackintosh. Thatchers use different styles and patterns for ridging and finishing their work, in different parts of the country, and some will incorporate their own special patterns as a kind of trademark. It takes about 3 weeks in decent weather to thatch a medium-sized cottage, not long enough to get bored !

Beef and Potato Layer Pie

serves 4

1½ lb [750 g] **potatoes, thinly
   sliced**
1½ lb [750 g] **minced beef**
2 oz [50 g] **butter**
1 clove **garlic, chopped**
2 medium **onions, chopped**
8 oz [250 g] **tomatoes, chopped**
3 teaspoons [3×5 ml spoons]
   parsley, chopped
a pinch of **thyme**
½ pint [250 ml] **cheese sauce**
salt and pepper

Fry the meat lightly in a little of
the butter, then remove from the
pan.
Add the remaining butter and fry
the garlic and onion gently for 5
minutes.
Stir in the tomatoes, parsley,
thyme and seasoning, continuing
cooking until the mixture is quite
soft.
Return the meat to the tomato
mixture.
Butter a round pie dish and cover
the base with overlapping slices of
raw potato.
Fill up with alternate layers of
meat, potato, finishing with
potato.
Pour over the sauce and bake at
375°F (190°), Gas Mark 5, for
1 hour.

Hereford Rissoles

serves 4

1½ lb [750 g] **potatoes**
1½ lb [750 g] **raw minced chuck
   steak**
1 small **onion, minced**
1 level teaspoon [1×5 ml spoon]
   paprika pepper
dash of **Worcestershire sauce**
1 beaten **egg**
a little **flour**
oil
salt and pepper

Mix together the beef, onion,
paprika pepper, sauce, salt, and
egg, with enough flour to bind the
mixture.
Shape small cakes and coat with
seasoned flour.
Fry the cakes in ¼ inch (0.5 cm)
oil, turning them over until
completely golden brown.
Boil the potatoes, drain them
well, and dry over a low heat with
the pan lid off to make the
potatoes floury.
Press them through a ricer to
make a border on a flat serving
dish.
Pile the rissoles in the centre and
coat, if liked, with a rich gravy or
fresh tomato sauce.

Beef Fillets - Country Style

serves 4

1 lb [500 g] **potatoes**
1 lb [500 g] **thick rump steak**
8 oz [250 g] **mushrooms**
oil
½ pint [250 ml] **brown stock**
1 tablespoon [1×20 ml spoon]
   horseradish sauce
1 tablespoon [1×20 ml spoon]
   redcurrant jelly
3 or 4 **peppercorns**
parsley
salt and pepper

Scoop the potatoes into balls and
cook in boiling salted water until
tender.
Simmer together for 15 minutes
the stock, horseradish, redcurrant
jelly and peppercorns.
Cut the steak into pieces and
season with salt and pepper and
fry in the hot oil until tender.
Sauté the mushrooms separately.
Pile the potato balls in the centre
of the dish, surround with the
mushrooms and steak. Strain the
gravy and pour over the meat.
Garnish the potatoes with
chopped parsley.

It was said that if you saw a hay
wagon, you should make a wish,
and to be even more sure of its
coming true, first count up to
thirteen.

Oxtail and Potato Stew

serves 4

1½ lb [750g] **potatoes, cut into large cubes**
2½ lb [1¼ kg] **oxtail**
1 oz [25 g] **butter**
1 **large onion, sliced**
1 **medium carrot, sliced**
½ **a small turnip, diced**
1 **bay leaf** ⎤
6 **peppercorns** ⎬ **tied in muslin**
3 **cloves** ⎦
¾ **pint** [375 ml] **boiling water**
2 **level tablespoons** [2×20 ml spoons] **flour**
3 **tablespoons** [3×20 ml spoons] **water**
1 **dessertspoon** [1×10 ml spoon] **vinegar**
pepper
1 **teaspoon** [1×5 ml spoon] **salt**

Remove any excess fat from oxtail.

Melt the butter in a large pan, add the onion and fry till golden.

Add the oxtail and carrot and turnip, and fry briskly for 5 minutes.

Add the herbs, boiling water and salt and pepper.

Simmer for approximately 3 hours till the meat is very tender (almost falling away from the bone).

Remove the muslin bag. Leave overnight in a cool place.

Remove fat from the surface of the pan.

Add the potatoes and bring to the boil and simmer gently for approx. 15-20 minutes till the potatoes are cooked.

Blend the flour with the water and vinegar, and add to the pan, stirring until it boils and the liquid thickens.

Garnish with freshly chopped parsley.

RED DEAD NETTLE.

Colonial Stew

serves 4

1½ lb [750 g] **potatoes**
2 lb [1 kg] **salt beef**
2 **carrots**
2 **turnips**
4 **onions**
1 small **cabbage**
2 small **beetroot**
salt and pepper

Place the beef in cold water, bring to the boil and skim.
Simmer for 2 hours.
Add the prepared vegetables, except the cabbage, and simmer for a further hour.
Add the shredded cabbage and continue cooking for 15 minutes.
Boil the beetroot separately, peel and dice them, and combine with the stew when serving.

Meat Loaf

serves 4

1 lb [500 g] **potatoes, grated**
1 lb [500 g] **minced steak, lean**
8 oz [250 g] **minced bacon, lean**
1 large **onion, grated**
1 tablespoon [1×20 ml spoon] **parsley, chopped**
1 **egg, beaten**
salt and pepper

Grate the potato into a bowl and pour off excess water.
Add the steak, bacon, onion, parsley, salt and pepper and mix thoroughly with the egg.
Place in a greased bowl and press down well.
Cover with foil and place in a pan of boiling water.
Boil gently for 2½-3 hours and allow to cool before turning out.
Serve with mixed salad.

Potato Volcano

serves 4

2 lb [1 kg] **potatoes, mashed with a knob of butter**
a little milk
1 **onion, chopped**
1 oz [25 g] **butter**
1 lb [500 g] **minced beef**
1 **can condensed vegetable soup**
½ **cup water**
parsley, chopped
salt and pepper

Beat the potatoes with butter and milk until creamy.
Fry the onion in the butter.
Add the minced beef and fry till brown, then add the soup and water and simmer for 20 minutes. Adjust the seasoning.
Pile the potatoes on a large dish, making a hollow in the centre.
Pour the mince into the hollow and serve immediately, sprinkled with the chopped parsley.

Windmills

Once from almost any high place in England you could see the turning sails of many windmills twirling away. In the wetlands there were rows of them pumping water out of the marshes. These turning sails were as familiar a part of life as they had been since the 12th century from when the first records of windmills date.

More efficient steam powered roller mills finished corn windmills by the 1930s and mechanical pumps replaced the drainage windmills. Most windmills were demolished but plenty of survivors have been restored to working order, or at least saved from total destruction, particularly in East Anglia and the South East.

All windmills work through a series of gear wheels. The sails are on an axle or 'windshaft' which carries an enormous toothed 'brake wheel'. Geared to this wheel is a 'wallower' on a vertical shaft; at the bottom of this is the 'great spur wheel' which drives a smaller gear, a 'stone nut' on a spindle, turning the 'runner millstones' suspended just above the 'bed stone'. The grain is fed between the stones and passes out into a machine which sifts the flour from the bran.

In pumping mills the great spur wheel drives a 'pit wheel' on a horizontal axle on the other end of which is a scoop wheel to move the water.

The oldest type is the post mill in which the wooden body pivots on an enormous post held in place by a trestle, and is rotated by hand or by a fantail to face into the wind. Brick tower mills have a wooden cap on top to carry the sails and windshaft, and a fantail at the back to turn it into the wind. Smock mills, which look a little like a countryman in a smock, are like tower mills, but the whole mill is made of weatherboarding on a wooden framework.

Wallcott Pie

Potato and Sausage Roll

serves 4

1 lb [500 g] **new potatoes**
1 large onion, chopped finely
2 oz [50 g] **mushrooms, sliced**
8 oz [250 g] **steak mince**
10½ oz **can condensed tomato**
   soup
Worcestershire sauce
butter
salt and pepper

Scrub or scrape the potatoes and
parboil for 5 minutes.
Fry the onion and mushrooms in
butter until soft.
Add the mince and brown
slightly.
Add the soup, a few drops of
sauce, season and bring to the
boil.
Turn into a greased casserole.
Slice the potatoes to ¼ inch
(0.5 cm) thick and place on the
meat, overlapping the slices.
Brush over with a little melted
butter and bake at 350°F
(180°C), Gas Mark 4, for 35
minutes.

serves 4

8 oz [250 g] **potatoes, cooked and**
   diced
1 lb [500 g] **beef sausage meat**
2 eggs, hardboiled and chopped
3 oz [75 g] **Cheddar cheese,**
   grated
1 teaspoon [1×5 ml spoon] **mixed**
   herbs
1 egg, beaten
salt and pepper

Place the potatoes, eggs, cheese,
and herbs in a bowl and add
sufficient egg to bind. Season with
salt and pepper.
Roll out the sausage meat on a
floured board into an oblong of
about ¼ inch (0.5 cm) thick.
Place on a sheet of lightly greased
foil.
Spread the filling over the meat.
Roll up and brush with beaten
egg.
Loosely cover with foil and bake
at 375°F (190°C), Gas Mark 5,
for 30 minutes.
Turn back the foil and cook for a
further 20 minutes.

It is hard to believe in the
eating capacities of some of our
ancestors. A famous figure like
King Edward VII springs readily
to mind, but there are many
accounts by lesser folk of pro-
digious feats of eating. The diarist
James Woodforde, a humble
country parson living in Suffolk in
the second half of the eighteenth
century describes many a hearty
meal of which this is one of the
more exotic examples: 'We had
for dinner a Calf's Head, boiled
Fowl and Tongue, a saddle of
mutton rosted on the Side Table
and a fine Swan rosted with
currant Jelly sauce for the first
course. The second course a
couple of wild fowl called Dun
Fowls, Larks, Blamange, Tarts
etc etc and a good desert of Fruits
after amongst which was a
Damson Cheese. I never eat a bit
of a Swan before and I think it
good eating with sweet sauce. The
Swan was killed 3 weeks before it
was eat and yet not the least bad
taste in it.'

Brisket Stew

Beef Rolls

'A swarm of bees in May
  Is worth a load of hay
A swarm of bees in June
  Is worth a silver spoon
A swarm of bees in July
  Is not worth a butterfly.'

serves 4

3 lb [1½ kg] **potatoes, diced**
2 lb [1 kg] **brisket of beef**
1 teaspoon [1×5 ml spoon] **salt**
1½ pints [750 ml] **water**
2 lb [1 kg] **carrots, diced**
1 lb [500 g] **onions, chopped**
salt and pepper

Place the beef in a large pan of salted water. Bring to the boil and skim. Simmer for 1½ hours.
Add the carrots, and cook for a further 30 minutes, then add the potatoes and onions.
Continue cooking until the meat is tender and vegetables very soft.
Remove the meat and vegetables from the pan and keep warm in a serving dish.
Boil the liquid briskly until most has evaporated. Check the seasoning.
Pour over the meat and vegetables and serve piping hot.

serves 4

12 oz [375 g] **beef, lean and thinly sliced (silverside or topside)**
butter
flour
1 cut clove garlic
water
¼ pint [125 ml] **red wine**
Stuffing:
4 oz [100 g] **potato, mashed**
1 teaspoon [1×5 ml spoon] **parsley, chopped**
2 mushrooms, chopped
2 rashers bacon, chopped
salt and pepper

Rub the beef slices with garlic and sprinkle with freshly ground pepper.
Mix together the ingredients for the stuffing and place some on each beef slice.
Roll up and tie each one with string.
Coat with seasoned flour and fry all over in melted butter.
Strain off any excess butter and stir in the wine with just enough water to cover the meat.
Cover the pan and cook very gently for 1-1½ hours.

Golden Tripe Fritters

serves 4

2 lb [1 kg] **potatoes, sieved or riced**
2 oz [50 g] **butter**
a little milk
1 lb [500 g] **tripe, cooked**
1 egg
1 teacup flour
½ cup milk
salt and pepper
fat for frying

Beat the potatoes thoroughly with butter and milk.
Place on a deep plate, bringing the potato up the sides.
Cover the potato base with foil.
Cook in a hot oven at 400°F (200°C), Gas Mark 6, till the edge and sides are firm and golden brown.
Sieve the flour into a bowl, make a well in the centre and add the egg and milk. Beat till smooth.
Dip pieces of tripe into the batter and deep fry until golden.
Stand fritters upright on the bed of potatoes.

Herbal medicine continues to fascinate, and many traditional cures are still prepared by country folk. To quote just a few, an infusion of blackcurrant leaves is good for stomach pains, and is also used as a tonic. Mint tea before retiring is a calmative and sleep-inducer. Lavender oil well rubbed in is good for sprains. A cabbage leaf placed on the forehead will help to chase away a headache. The pungent onion is used in soup for colds and bad chests, and crushed onion with a pinch of salt is soothing to burns. An attractive sounding laxative is made from a syrup of violets, while sore eyes can be comforted by bathing them in rosewater.

Garden Mint

Beef and Lentil Casserole

serves 4

1 lb [500 g] **potatoes, thinly sliced**
4 oz [100 g] **lentils**
4 oz [100 g] **stewing steak**
8 oz [250 g] **carrot, turnip, or swede, diced**
4 oz [100 g] **onion, sliced**
water
salt and pepper

Wash the lentils thoroughly, soak overnight, transfer to a pan, boil, and simmer gently for 5 minutes.
Cut the meat into small pieces and place on the base of a greased dish. Cover with lentils and water, and season.
Add the vegetables and season, making sure the water comes half way up the dish.
Arrange the potatoes to overlap. Cover with a lid or foil and cook for 2 hours at 350°F (180°C), Gas Mark 4.
Uncover, and brown in the oven for a further 10-15 minutes.

Nettle Beer

Choose 2 gallons of young nettles. Wash and put into a saucepan with 2 gallons of water, ½ oz. root ginger, 4 lbs. malt, 2 ozs. hops and 4 ozs. sarsaparilla. Bring to the boil and boil for ¼ hour; put 1½ lbs. castor sugar into a large pan or earthenware jar; strain nettle mixture on to it. Stir until sugar has dissolved. Beat 1 oz. yeast to a cream, and add, leaving until it begins to ferment; then put into bottles. Cork and tie down with string. This may be used at once.

Recipe reprinted
from Farmhouse Fare

Tripe and Potato Hotpot

serves 4

2 lb [1 kg] **potatoes**
1 lb [500 g] **tripe**
1 lb [500 g] **onions, sliced**
1 oz [25 g] **plain flour**
butter
stock
salt and pepper

Wash the tripe and cut into small pieces. Dip in seasoned flour.
Peel and slice the potatoes.
Grease a casserole with butter.
Place all the ingredients in layers, seasoning each one to taste. Make the top layer of potatoes.
Pour over the stock to half fill the dish.
Place a few knobs of butter on top potatoes. Cover and bake at 375°F (190°C), Gas Mark 5, for 1-1½ hours.
Remove the lid for the last 10 minutes cooking time to brown the top.

Potato Beef Goulash

serves 4

1 large **onion, chopped**
1 lb [500 g] **chuck steak, cut into strips**
1½ lb [750 g] **potatoes, peeled and thinly sliced**
1 level tablespoon [1×20 ml spoon] **paprika pepper**
1 level tablespoon [1×20 ml spoon] **tomato purée**
2 fl oz [50 ml] **cooking oil**
½ teaspoon [2.5 ml] **vinegar**
a pinch of marjoram
½ pint [250 ml] **water**
salt

Fry the onions in oil till golden.
Add the paprika and stir well.
Add the meat, cover, and allow to simmer for 5 minutes.
Add the water, purée, salt, vinegar and marjoram.
Line the sides and base of a greased casserole with potatoes, reserving some for the top. Place the meat in the casserole and the remaining potatoes (overlapping) on top.
Cover and cook in oven at 325°F (170°C), Gas Mark 3, for 2-2½ hours.
Remove lid about 20 minutes before end of cooking time to allow potatoes to crisp and brown.

Seville Veal with Crispy Fries

serves 4

Crispy Fries
1 lb [500 g] **potatoes, peeled**
1 teaspoon [1×5 ml spoon] **thyme**
salt and pepper
1 lb [500 g] **veal fillets**
2 oz [50 g] **butter**
Sauce
2 oz [50 g] **butter**
2 oz [50 g] **soft brown sugar**
1 fresh orange, rind removed and sliced
½ pint [250 ml] **fresh orange juice**

Beat veal fillets with rolling pin till very thin.
Place in melted butter and fry gently on both sides until cooked.
Drain and keep hot on serving dish.
Make sauce by melting the butter and sugar in a pan.
Fry the orange slices in this syrup for 3 minutes then add the orange juice.
Simmer gently for about 30 minutes.
To make the crispy fries grate the potato into a bowl. Pour off any excess water.
Add thyme, salt and pepper, mix well together.
Place sufficient oil in the pan, just covering the base and no more.
Drop dessertspoons (10 ml spoons) into oil, flatten with back of a spoon until very thin.
Fry on both sides for 5-8 minutes.
Place the crispy fries around the veal and pour the sauce over the veal fillets.

He that would live for aye
Must eat Sage in May.

Old English

Veal and Potato Layer

serves 4

2 lb [1 kg] **potatoes, sieved or riced**
2 oz [50 g] **butter**
2½ fl oz [62 ml] **milk**
nutmeg
brown breadcrumbs
salt and pepper
Filling:
1 lb [500 g] **stewing veal, diced**
1 oz [25 g] **butter**
1 medium onion, finely chopped
1 teaspoon [1×5 ml spoon] **sage**
1 lemon, peel only
½ glass water
salt and pepper

For the filling, melt the butter in a pan and fry the onion gently till pale gold.
Add the veal and fry briskly for a few minutes.
Add the sage, grated lemon peel, water, and salt and pepper.
Cook till the meat is tender and all the liquid has evaporated.
Add the butter, salt and pepper and nutmeg to the potatoes, mixing well.
Grease an 8 inch (20 cm), loose bottom, tin with butter and coat with breadcrumbs.
Place half the potatoes into the tin and smooth over.
Place the veal over the potatoes and brush with a little melted butter. Cover with remaining potatoes.
Place in the oven and cook at 375°F (190°C), Gas Mark 5, for 40 minutes.

Veal, Apple, Potato Casserole

serves 4

1 lb [500 g] **potatoes, peeled and sliced**
1 lb [500 g] **lean stewing veal**
1 oz [25 g] **seasoned flour**
1 oz [25 g] **butter**
1 **onion, skinned and sliced**
8 oz [250 g] **cooking apples**
1 teaspoon [1×5 ml spoon] **sugar**
½ pint [250 ml] **chicken stock**
5 oz [125 g] **sour cream**
salt and pepper

Cut the veal into 2 inch (5 cm) cubes and coat in seasoned flour.
Melt the butter in a pan, add the veal and brown, then add the onions and cook all for a further 2 minutes.
Add the apples, reserving one unpeeled apple for garnishing, remove the cores, and slice into rings.
Place these on top of the casserole, pressing gently into the stock, sprinkle with sugar.
Cover and cook in a slow oven, 325°F (170°C), Gas Mark 3, for 1½ hours. Just before serving, spoon on soured cream and garnish with thinly sliced apple.

Spinach Potatoes with Veal

serves 4

12 oz [375 g] **potatoes**
1 **small packet frozen spinach, chopped**
1 oz [25 g] **butter**
1½ lb [750 g] **veal cutlets**
2 oz [50 g] **butter**
¼ pint [125 ml] **single cream**

Cook the potatoes and mash them.
Beat in the butter until creamy.
Add the cooked spinach and mix well.
Serve piped as a border round an oval dish.
Melt butter in a frying pan.
Gently fry the fillets until cooked.
Pour over the single cream and allow to heat without boiling.
Place fillets and sauce in the centre of the potato border. Serve immediately.

Pork and Apple Pie

serves 4

Potato Pastry:
8 oz [250 g] **potatoes, sieved or riced**
4 oz [100 g] **plain flour**
2 oz [50 g] **butter**
½ teaspoon [2.5 ml] **baking powder**
water to mix
a pinch of salt
Filling:
1½ lb [750 g] **leg of pork, coarsely chopped into shreds**
12 oz [375 g] **apples**
sugar
1 **onion, small**
a little white stock
salt and pepper

Place a layer of meat in a deep greased casserole and cover with a layer of roughly chopped apples. Dust with sugar.
Grate a small onion over this and season.
Repeat layers until all ingredients have been used. Pack down well.
Add a little stock, barely enough to moisten.
Cover with a thick crust of potato pastry.
Knock up the edges and flute, make leaves with pastry to decorate.
Bake in a slow oven, 300°F (150°C), Gas Mark 2.
for 1½ hours.
To make the potato pastry:
Rub the butter into the flour.
Add the baking powder and salt and thoroughly blend into the potatoes.
Add sufficient water to form a stiff dough.

Potato, Sausage and Bacon Pie

serves 4

1 lb [500 g] **potatoes, peeled**
    boiled and riced
1 lb [500 g] **pork sausages**
4 oz [100 g] **bacon pieces**
2 tablespoons [2×20 ml spoons]
    tomato purée
½-¾ pint [250-375 ml] **stock**
1 oz [25 g] **flour**
a pinch of mixed herbs
1 egg
3 bay leaves
salt and pepper

Fry or grill the sausages lightly till
almost cooked and remove from
the frying pan.
Fry the bacon pieces lightly, stir
in the flour, then slowly add the
stock to make a sauce. Add the
tomato purée.
Beat the egg and herbs in to the
potato.
Place the sausage in the centre of
an oblong ovenproof dish, pour
the sauce over, then pipe a border
of mashed potato around the
dish.
Bake in oven 375°F (190°C), Gas
Mark 5, for 20-25 minutes.
Garnish with bay leaves.

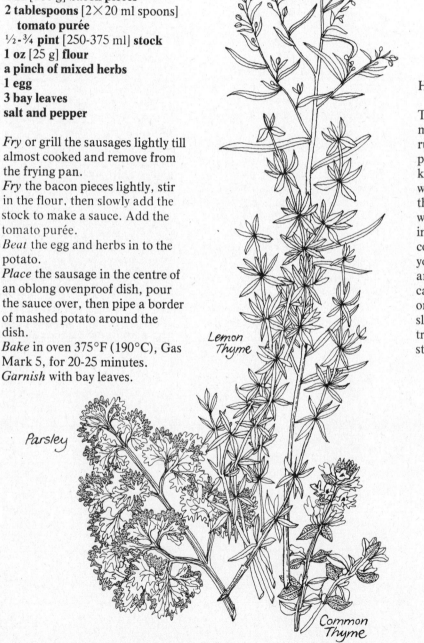

Tarragon

Lemon Thyme

Parsley

Common Thyme

Herb Window Box

This week I have been lifting my
mint, thyme, parsley, borage and
rue and planting them in a gaily
painted window box, for my
kitchen window-sill. Ordinary soil
will do, keeping it moist. I shall
then have a supply of herbs for the
winter, even if you still have some
in the garden it's often too wet or
cold to run out. Incidentally, if
your garden mint tends to run
amok, to prevent it spreading you
can dig a hole and sink a large tin
or washing up bowl, leaving it
slightly above soil level, and if you
transplant your mint to this it will
stay put.

Mrs. Sangster

Potato and Courgette Bake

serves 4

1 lb [500 g] **potatoes, peeled and sliced thickly**
8 oz [250 g] **courgettes**
4 **bacon chops**
1 **small can apricots**
1 tablespoon [1×20 ml spoon] **demerara sugar**

Parboil the potatoes for 3-4 minutes and drain.
Cut the courgettes in half lengthwise and parboil.
Grease an ovenproof casserole, cover with the potatoes and place the courgettes on top; then place the bacon chops over the vegetables.
Arrange the apricots around the side of the dish, pour over the fruit juice and sprinkle the sugar over the bacon.
Cook in a moderate oven, 350°F (180°C), Gas Mark 4, for 30-40 minutes.

Southern Style Pork

serves 4

2 lb [1 kg] **roast flank pork ready for stuffing and rolling**
Stuffing:
8 oz [250 g] **potato, mashed**
8 oz [250 g] **pork sausage meat**
rind of one orange
2 oz [50 g] **sultanas**
1 dessertspoon [1×10 ml spoon] **redcurrant jelly**
1 **onion, lightly fried**
yolk of an egg
salt and pepper

Bind all the stuffing ingredients together, season, and spread over the centre of the meat to within one inch of the edges.
Roll up the roast and secure with string.
Cover with foil and cook in a moderate oven, 375°F (190°C), Gas Mark 5, for 1½ hours.
If you are making gravy to serve with this, try adding to it the juice of ½ an orange and a tablespoon (1×20 ml spoon) of redcurrant jelly.

Country Ham

serves 4

1 lb [500 g] **potatoes, boiled**
1 **small onion, finely chopped**
2 oz [50 g] **mushrooms, chopped**
2 **skinned tomatoes**
½ oz [12.5 g] **flour**
¼ pint [125 ml] **milk**
1 teaspoon [1×5 ml spoon] **chutney**
8 oz [250 g] **cooked ham, chopped**
salt and pepper

Fry the onion in butter till lightly browned.
Add the mushrooms and tomatoes and cook for a few minutes.
Add the flour and mix well, then gradually add the milk and bring to the boil.
Add the chutney, ham and seasoning and place in a greased ovenproof dish.
Slice the potatoes to about ¼ inch (0.5 cm) thick and place over the mixture, overlapping the slices. Brush with butter and bake at 400°F (200°C), Gas Mark 6, for 20 minutes.

That keen observer and tireless rural rider, William Cobbett noted, 'When the wheat or grain has to ripen in wet weather, it will not be so bright as it will when it has to ripen in fair weather. It will have a dingy and clouded appearance, and perhaps the flour might not be quite so good.'

Baked Gammon Potatoes

serves 6

8 oz-12 oz [250-375 g] **gammon or bacon, cooked and diced**
6 **large potatoes**
1 **large onion, finely chopped**
2 **teaspoons** [2×5 ml spoons] **made French mustard**
3 oz [75 g] **butter**
cream, or top of milk
Cheddar cheese, grated
salt and pepper
1 **egg**

Scrub the potatoes, dry them and prick the skins in several places.
Rub a little butter into the skins.
Place on a baking sheet and cook until soft in oven 425°F (220°C), Gas Mark 7.
Fry the onion in a little butter until cooked, add the bacon or gammon, and stir well together. Keep warm.
Slice the potatoes in half and scoop out the centres into a bowl.
Mash with the remaining butter and add the mustard, seasoning, bacon and onion.
Mix in a little cream.
Add the egg and beat in well while the mixture is still hot.
Pile the filling into the potato jackets and sprinkle with grated cheese.
Reheat in hot oven 425°F (220°C), Gas Mark 7, for 10 minutes.

Sweet and Sour Hotpot

serves 4

1½ lb [750 g] **potatoes**
4 oz [100 g] **bacon, lean**
1 **onion**
1 oz [25 g] **plain flour**
1 oz [25 g] **butter**
½ **pint** [250 ml] **light stock**
1 **tablespoon** [1×20 ml spoon] **wine vinegar**
1 **teaspoon** [1×5 ml spoon] **sugar**
8 oz [250 g] **French beans**
salt and pepper

Prepare the potatoes, boil them until just cooked, and cut into slices about ¼ inch (0.5 cm) thick.
Cut the bacon into small pieces and slice the onion. Fry gently in the butter for a few minutes until both begin to cook.
Sprinkle in the flour, stir, and cook gently without browning, then gradually add the stock, stirring until boiling.
To this, add the sliced potatoes, vinegar, sugar, salt and pepper to taste.
Trim the beans and cut and add them to the dish.
Cover the dish and simmer for 30 minutes.
A decorative cooker-to-table pan or casserole is an ideal container for this colourful dish.

Madeleine's Pork Pie

serves 4

1 lb [500 g] **potatoes, mashed**
1 lb [500 g] **carrots, mashed or purée**
1 oz [25 g] **butter**
Filling:
12 oz [375 g] **pig's liver, shredded or coarsely grated**
12 oz [375 g] **pork sausage meat**
2 **onions, chopped**
1 oz [25 g] **butter**
2 **level tablespoons** [2×20 ml spoons] **flour**
¼ **pint** [125 ml] **beef stock**
2 **tablespoons** [2×20 ml spoons] **Worcestershire sauce**
milk
salt and pepper

Pour sufficient milk over the liver to cover and set aside for 30 minutes, then drain and mince coarsely or shred.
Fry the onion in butter till transparent and soft. Add the liver and brown.
Add the sausage meat, flour and stock, sauce and seasoning, and mix well together.
Place in a greased casserole.
Place the potatoes, carrots and butter into a bowl and beat till smooth.
Place in a piping bag with star nozzle and pipe the mixture over the meat.
Glaze with a little melted butter.
Cook in a hot oven at 400°F (200°C), Gas Mark 6, for 30 minutes till golden brown.

Water Diviners

A water diviner at work is watched by at best, the sceptical, and at worst those who suspect him (or her) of witchcraft. About one in five people possess the power to receive electromagnetic impulses from flowing water which translate themselves into physical movement of whatever type of divining rod the 'dowser' is using. There is no full scientific explanation of this indisputable power. The professional dowser practices his art until by long experience, and taking a series of readings over an area, he can tell how much water there is and how deep it is. Very difficult to explain is the power some dowsers have to divine over large scale maps by holding a bob or pendulum. As it oscillates it enables the dowser to pinpoint working areas before he gets out into the field.

Make some divining rods by taking two pieces of brazing rod (from a garage or smithy), bend them down at right angles 3 inches in from the end. With elbows at sides, hold the rods loosely by the short ends, one in each fist, pointing forwards. Walk along concentrating your mind on water, and when you are above a supply the rods will swing together and cross.

A forked hazel twig fresh cut and sappy, held in the fists with the thumbs upwards will jump or dip for some diviners. The trick is to find the point where the twig is exactly cocked, then any change of tension will cause it to spring up or down. The impulse which the diviner receives causes slight involuntary muscle movement in the hands which twists the twig, and may even cause a tingling sensation. Even the top thin section of a fly fishing rod will oscillate when held pointing down at the ground just above a water supply.

Pippin Pie

serves 4

12 oz [375 g] **potatoes, raw**
1 lb [500 g] **pork without bone**
2 Cox's Orange Pippin apples
1 onion, large
¼ pint [125 ml] **dry cider**
1 chicken stock cube
1 packet frozen puff pastry
1 oz [25 g] **butter**
2 oz [50 g] **seasoned flour**
salt and pepper

Cube the pork in ½ inch (1 cm) cubes and toss in the seasoned flour, coating liberally.
Peel and cube the apple, dice the potatoes and slice the onion.
Fry the onion lightly in the butter, add the diced potatoes and cubed apple and fry for a further few minutes. Remove from the pan.
Turn up the heat and brown the pork in the frying pan. When browned, crumble the stock cube over the meat and pour in the dry cider, scraping down any sediment from the sides and bottom of the pan.
Put the potatoes, apples and onions back in beside the meat, mixing everything together and seasoning if necessary.
Turn in to a pie dish and cover with the puff pastry.
Bake at 425°F (220°C), Gas Mark 7, for 20 minutes and then at 350°F (180°C), Gas Mark 4, for a further 40 minutes.

Potato Pork de Luxe

serves 4

2 lb [1 kg] **potatoes, peeled and thinly sliced**
1 lb [500 g] **cooking apples, peeled and cut into rings**
1 can condensed cream of mushroom soup
4 tablespoons [4×20 ml spoons] **sour cream**
2 tablespoons [2×20 ml spoons] **water**
4 pork chops
2 tablespoons [2×20 ml spoons] **parsley, chopped**
salt and pepper

Place a layer of potato slices in a greased ovenproof dish.
Cover with the apple rings, salt and pepper.
Blend the soup, sour cream, water and parsley.
Pour the soup mixture over the apples.
Arrange a layer of overlapping potato slices on top.
Melt the fat in the frying pan and fry the pork quickly to brown.
Place the pork chops on top of the potato, and cover with a lid or a piece of aluminium foil.
Cook in a moderate hot oven, 375°F (190°C), Gas Mark 5, for 1-1¼ hours and sprinkle with parsley.

Devilled Pork Hotpot

serves 4

1 lb [500 g] **potatoes, peeled**
4 **pork chops**
1 large **cooking apple, peeled and sliced**
1 teaspoon [1×5 ml spoon] **Worcestershire sauce**
a few drops **tabasco sauce**
1 large **onion, sliced**
½ **pint** [250 ml] **white wine**
1 oz [25 g] **butter**
1 teaspoon [1×5 ml spoon] **made mustard**

Melt the butter in a frying pan and brown the chops on both sides.
Cover a greased casserole with half the quantity of potatoes, sprinkle with lemon juice, and place the chops on top.
Cover the chops with a layer of apples.
Mix together the Worcestershire sauce, tabasco, white wine and mustard, chutney and seasoning, and pour over the chops, then cover the dish with the remaining potatoes and onions.
Brush with melted butter.
Cover and cook at 375°F (190°C), Gas Mark 5, for approx. 1½ hours. The lid can be removed after 1 hour to allow the potatoes to brown.

Festive Lamb with Fantail Potatoes

serves 6-8

1 small **leg of lamb**
1 clove of **garlic**
2 tablespoons [2×20 ml spoons] **honey**
2 **pineapple rings**
4-5 **cocktail cherries and cocktail sticks**
salt and pepper

Wipe the lamb, cut the garlic into pieces and insert into bone.
Sprinkle with salt and pepper.
Cook for 25 minutes per 1 lb (500 g) meat. Cooking temperature: 375°F (190°C), Gas Mark 5.
Glaze the lamb with honey 15 minutes before serving. Remove garlic. Decorate with pineapple and cherries.
Serve with fantail potatoes.

Fantail potatoes
2 lb [1 kg] **potatoes, peeled**
½ **pint** [250 ml] **milk**
4 oz [100 g] **butter**

Cut a thin slice from the bottom of each potato so that they will stand level.
Cut into ¼ in (0.5 cm) slices, about halfway through potatoes.
Place on a greased ovenproof dish. Pour in milk, season and dot with butter.
Bake in a hot oven, basting occasionally, at 400°F (200°C), Gas Mark 6, for 1-1¼ hours.
When half-cooked, pinch each potato gently so that the slices will open out.
Serve as an accompaniment to meat or savoury dishes.

Lamb Chop Crunch

serves 4

1 lb [500 g] **potatoes**
1 medium **onion**
¼ **pint** [125 ml] **stock or water**
4 **loin chops**
1 tablespoon [1×20 ml spoon] **oatmeal**
a little **oil**
salt and pepper

Peel and slice the potato and chop the onion finely.
Sprinkle the onion and seasoning among layers of potato slices.
Pour over the stock.
Dip the chops in the oatmeal and brown on both sides in hot oil.
Remove from the pan and place on top of the potatoes.
Bake at 375°F (190°C), Gas Mark 5, for 1-1½ hours.

Thanksgiving

For apples, yellow, green and red,
  Among the leaves, above my
  head;
For luscious plums, a-drip with
  juice
  Awaiting jam for winter use;
For lettuce green and full of heart
  Playing salad's better part;
For peas, with pods a-popping
  fast,
  With lamb and mint sauce -
  good repast;
For beans a-hanging in their
  grove,
  Bunched high and low or
  interwove;
For potatoes in surprising store-
  Spade signalling to dig up
  more!
For beetroot purple, swollen
  round,
  Beneath expansive foliage
  found;
For onions on the surface sitting,
  Spikes o'ertipped - in sockets
  fitting;
For carrots, turnips, swedes in
  rows,
  To taste the stew when raw
  wind blows;
For cauliflower in splendid state-
  A produce posy of some weight;
For Brassica of every kind-
  Savoy and Brussel - Kale
  behind;
For all things come to their full
  fruit
  From highest tree to lowest
  root.

                                    T.E.

Mint Lamb Pie

serves 4

1½ lb [750 g] **neck of lamb**
1 oz [25 g] **seasoned flour**
1 tablespoon [1×20 ml spoon]
  cooking oil
Filling:
1 lb [500 g] **tiny new
  potatoes**
1 **medium onion, chopped**
2 level tablespoons [2×20 ml
  spoons] **mint, chopped**
4 oz [100 g] **carrots, scraped and
  sliced**
4 oz [100 g] **fresh peas**
1 pkt 7½ oz [225 g] **flaky pastry**
milk or egg to glaze
½ pint [250 ml] **beef stock**
salt and pepper

Cut the lamb into 1 inch (2.5 cm)
cubes and toss in the flour.
Heat the oil in a pan and fry the
onion gently for 3 minutes.
Add the lamb and cook for a
further 5 minutes.
Add the potatoes, stock and mint
and bring to the boil.
Simmer for 35 minutes, add the
carrots and peas, and cook for a
further 10 minutes.
Turn into a 2 pint (1 litre) pie
dish.
Cover the pie with the pastry,
knock up the edges and flute.
Roll out any trimmings and cut
into leaves to decorate.
Brush with egg or milk and make
a slit in the pastry.
Bake at 400°F (200°C), Gas
Mark 6, for 25-30 minutes till the
pastry is well risen and golden
brown.

Potato Moussaka

serves 4

1½ lb [750 g] **potatoes, thinly
  sliced**
12 oz [375 g] **fresh mince**
4 oz [100 g] **onion**
8 oz can **tomatoes**
2 oz [50 g] **butter**
parsley
salt and pepper
White Sauce:
1 oz [25 g] **butter**
1 oz [25 g] **flour**
½ pint [250 ml] **milk**
1 oz [25 g] **Cheddar cheese,
  grated**
1 **egg, beaten**
salt and pepper

Fry the meat, onions and
tomatoes in the butter.
Cover the base of a greased
casserole with overlapping potato
slices and season.
Cover with a layer of meat
mixture.
Repeat until all the ingredients
are used, finishing with a layer of
potato.
Add the beaten egg and cheese to
the white sauce and pour into the
casserole.
Bake at 375°F (190°C), Gas
Mark 5, for approximately 1
hour.
Sprinkle with chopped parsley.

King's Head Bake

serves 4

4 × 8-10 oz [250-300 g] **potatoes**
1½ oz [37 g] **butter**
4 **lamb kidneys cut into pieces**
1 **medium onion cut into rings**
2 tablespoons [2 × 20 ml spoons]
sherry
4 tablespoons [4 × 20 ml spoons]
cream
1 oz [25 g] **butter**
salt and pepper

Wash the potatoes, dry and prick
with a fork.
Bake at 425°F (220°C), Gas
Mark 7, for 1¼-1½ hours till
cooked.
Prepare the filling by frying the
kidneys and onion in butter till
cooked. Stir in the sherry and
cream but do not boil.
Remove a thin slice from the
potatoes and scoop out the potato
into a bowl and mash with butter,
salt and pepper.
Replace into skins, using a fork,
pressing against the sides and
over the top to form a collar,
leaving a hollow in the centre.
Pile in the kidney mixture and
return to oven for 10 minutes.

Sweetbread Nests

serves 4

1 lb [500 g] **potatoes, sieved or
riced**
1 oz [25 g] **butter**
1 **egg**
1 **sweetbread**
¼ pint [250 ml] **white sauce**
1 **hard boiled egg, chopped**
milk and water
parsley, chopped
onion salt
pepper

Cook the sweetbread in milk and
water until tender.
Remove from the pan and break
down with a fork, taking out the
tissue.
Add to the sauce with hard boiled
egg and season with onion salt
and pepper.
Add the butter, egg and onion salt
to the potatoes and beat well.
Pipe the potatoes into nests and
bake at 425°F (220°C), Gas Mark
7, for 8-10 minutes.
Place the filling in the centres and
garnish with parsley.

Potato and Liver Scramble

serves 4

1 lb [500 g] **tiny new potatoes,
cooked**
8 oz [250 g] **lamb's liver, cut into
thin strips**
4 oz [100 g] **mushrooms**
3 **eggs**
¼ pint [125 ml] **milk**
1 oz [25 g] **butter**
2 oz [50 g] **Cheddar cheese,
grated**
salt and pepper

Melt the butter in a frying pan.
Add the potatoes, liver and
mushrooms and cook over a
gentle heat until the potatoes are
golden and the liver is cooked.
Beat the eggs with milk, salt and
pepper, and pour into a pan.
Keep moving the mixture around
with a fork until the egg is lightly
set, taking care not to overcook.
Sprinkle with cheese and place
under a hot grill till the cheese
bubbles.
Serve immediately, with a green
salad.

Potato Lamb Flan

serves 4

1½ lb [750 g] **potatoes, sieved or riced**
2 **egg yolks**
1 oz [25 g] **butter**
4 large or 8 small **lamb cutlets**
flour
cooking oil for frying
1 × 8 oz can **tomatoes**
1 tablespoon [1 × 20 ml] **tomato purée**
4 oz [100 g] **Cheddar cheese, cubed**
salt and pepper

Mix the potatoes with the egg yolks and butter, beating until smooth.
Grease a 9 inch (23 cm) ovenproof plate and pipe potatoes over the base and around the edge using a star nozzle.
Toss the chops in seasoned flour, then fry in a little oil on both sides to brown.
Arrange chops, overlapping them, on the bed of potato.
Mix the drained tomatoes with purée and cheese and spoon over the cutlets.
Cook in oven at 400°F (200°C), Gas Mark 6, for ½ an hour.

Logs to Burn

Read these lines and generally learn
  The proper kind of logs to burn.
Oak logs will warm you well
  If they're old and dry.
Larch logs like pinewood smell,
  But the sparks will fly.
Beech logs for Christmas-time,
  Yew logs heat well.
Scotch logs it is a crime
  For anyone to sell.
Birch logs will burn too fast,
  Chestnut scarce at all.
Hawthorn logs are good to last

If you cut them in the fall.
Holly logs will burn like wax,
  You should burn them green.
Elm logs like smouldering flax,
  No flames to be seen.
Pear logs and apple logs,
  They will scent your room.
Cherry logs across the dogs
  Will smell like flowers in bloom.
But ash logs, all smooth and grey,
  Burn them green or old;
Buy up all that comes your way,
  They're worth their weight in gold.

Old West Country Rhyme

Country Style Lamb

serves 4

1 lb [500 g] **potatoes, peeled and boiled**
1 lb [500 g] **cold leftover lamb**
2 tablespoons [2×20 ml spoons] **chutney or pickle**
cooking oil
onion sauce
salt and pepper
parsley, chopped

Line an ovenproof dish with thin slices of meat.
Spread over chutney or pickle and cover with thickly sliced potatoes.
Brush with oil and place in the oven to brown, 400°F (200°C) Gas Mark 6, for 25-30 minutes.
Serve with onion sauce, garnish with parsley.

Lamb's Liver Casserole

serves 4

1 lb [500 g] **potatoes, parboiled for 10 minutes**
1 lb [500 g] **lamb's liver**
1 large onion, finely chopped
1 tablespoon [1×20 ml spoon] **flour**
1 teaspoon [1×5 ml spoon] **powdered sage**
½ pint [250 ml] **stock or water**
salt and pepper

Toss the liver in seasoned flour.
Place half in a greased casserole.
Mix together the onion and sage and sprinkle half over the liver.
Repeat until all is used.
Add stock or water and cover with overlapping slices of potato.
Cook for one hour at 350°F (180°C), Gas Mark 4.

Lamb and Cabbage Hotpot

serves 4

2 lb [1 kg] **potatoes, peeled**
1 lb [500 g] **neck of lamb**
3 carrots, sliced
4 tablespoons [4×20 ml spoons]
  swede, diced
2 onions, large and thinly sliced
8 oz [250 g] **red cabbage**
  shredded
1 oz [25 g] **butter**
1 tablespoon [1×20 ml spoon]
  flour
a pinch of dried thyme
parsley, chopped
water or stock
salt and pepper

Melt the butter in a deep thick
based pan.
Mix together the flour, thyme,
salt and pepper, and toss the
lamb in the flour. Place in the pan
and quickly brown on both sides.
Add the cabbage, carrots, swede
and onions, pressing them well
down.
Cut 1 lb (500 g) of potatoes into
thin slices.
Place on top and season with salt
and pepper.
Add sufficient water, barely
covering, and then add the
remaining potatoes. (If small
keep whole, cut the larger ones in
half and place on top).
Cover with a closely fitting lid and
simmer very gently without
stirring, till cooked - about 1½ to
2 hours.
Sprinkle with parsley and serve
straight from the pan.

Stuffed Breast of Lamb

serves 4

1 breast of lamb, prepared
Stuffing:
1 lb [500 g] **potatoes**
4 oz [100 g] **pork sausage meat**
1 onion, chopped
2 celery stalks, finely chopped
paprika pepper
½ teaspoon [2.5 ml] **celery salt**
salt and pepper

Place the sausage meat in a pan
and stir over a gentle heat until
the fat runs. Remove from the
pan.
Add the onion to the fat in the
pan and fry till transparent but
not coloured.
Add the celery and cook for a
minute. Return the meat to pan.
Grate the potatoes, pouring off
the excess water, then add to
meat.
Season with celery salt, pepper
and paprika.
Cook gently for approx. 10
minutes, stirring frequently.
Allow the mixture to cool.
Spread the stuffing to within
1 inch (2.5 cm) of the edge of the
breast of lamb. Roll up and tie
securely with string.
Grease a large piece of foil lightly
and roll the breast of lamb in it.
Cook at 350°F (180°C), Gas
Mark 4, allowing 40 minutes to
the lb.

Lamb's Liver and Diced Potatoes

serves 4

1 lb [500 g] **potatoes**
1 lb [500 g] **lamb's liver, thinly sliced**
1 onion, very finely chopped
½ green pepper, finely chopped
2½ fl oz [65 ml] **fresh sour cream**
4 tablespoons [4×20 ml spoons] **red wine**
1 teaspoon [1×5 ml spoon] **paprika pepper**
2 oz [50 g] **butter**
salt and pepper

Cut the potatoes into ½ inch (1 cm) dice and boil for 3 minutes.
Melt the fat in a large frying pan.
Add the potatoes, turning frequently till they are golden brown. Lower the heat and add the onions and pepper and allow to cook without colouring. Remove from the pan.
Season the liver with salt and pepper.
Place in the frying pan, and when the liver blood starts to run turn over to the other side and cook for a few minutes more.
Return the vegetables to the pan, pour in the red wine and allow it to bubble and reduce a little.
Mix in the cream to make a sauce. Sprinkle with paprika.
Serve straight from the pan.

Sweet and Spicy Lamb's Kidneys

serves 4

1½ lb [750 g] **duchesse potatoes**
1 large onion, thinly sliced
1 oz [25 g] **butter**
8 lamb kidneys
4 oz [100 g] **mushrooms**
2 tablespoons [2×20 ml spoons] **H.P. sauce**
2 level teaspoons [2×5 ml spoons] **cornflour**
1 tablespoon [1×20 ml spoon] **redcurrant jelly**
salt and pepper

Fry the onion gently in butter for 5 minutes.
Cut the kidneys in half, remove the core and add to pan with mushrooms and fry for a further 5 minutes, sitrring occasionally.
Blend the cornflour with 1 tablespoon (1×20 ml spoon) water and add to the pan with sauce and jelly; season and cook for 5 minutes.
Pipe the potatoes round the edge of the serving dish to form a collar.
Place the kidneys in the centre.

Brecon Lamb

serves 4

1 lb [500 g] **potatoes**
8 oz [250 g] **leeks**
4 oz [100 g] **onions**
1 level dessertspoon [1×10 ml spoon] **cornflour**
12 oz [375 g] **stewing lamb**
1 teaspoon [1×5 ml spoon] **rosemary**
1 beef stock cube
¼ pint [125 ml] **water**
salt and pepper

Slice the potatoes thinly, chop the leeks and onion and mince the lamb. Put half the potatoes into the bottom of a casserole dish and then half of the leeks and onions.
Add the minced lamb and sprinkle with rosemary.
Place the remainder of the leeks and onions over the meat and finish with the remaining potatoes, seasoning as you go.
Mix the stock cube, cornflour and water together and pour over the ingredients in the casserole.
Cover the dish and bake for one hour at 400°f (200°C), Gas Mark 6.
Remove the lid and cook for a further half hour to brown the top layer of potatoes.

Lancashire Hotpot

Winter's Scene

No warmth, no cheerfulness, no
   healthful ease
   No comfortable feel in any
   member
No shade, no shine, no butterflies,
   no bees,
   No fruits, no flowers, no leaves,
   no birds - November.

serves 4

1-1½ lb [500-750 g] **potatoes,
   peeled**
1½ lb [750 g] **middle neck of
   lamb, trimmed**
2 sheep's kidneys
2 large onions, peeled
½ pint [250 ml] **stock**
butter
salt and pepper

Slice the potatoes thickly, slice the
onion and cut the lamb and
kidneys into neat pieces.
Place layers of the meat and
vegetables in a greased casserole,
season, and finish with a layer of
potatoes.
Add stock or water and cover with
the casserole lid or aluminium
foil.
Bake for about 2½ hours,
removing the lid for the last
½ hour to brown the potatoes,
325°F (170°C), Gas Mark 3.
Add small dabs of butter if the
potatoes get too dry during
cooking.
Serve with pickled red cabbage or
crumbled Lancashire cheese.

Almond Tart

serves 4

Potato Pastry:
4 oz [100 g] **self raising flour**
2 oz [50 g] **potatoes, sieved or riced**
3 oz [75 g] **butter**
water to bind
raspberry jam
a pinch of salt
Filling:
4 oz [100 g] **potatoes, sieved or riced**
2 oz [50 g] **butter**
2 oz [50 g] **castor sugar**
2 oz [50 g] **ground almonds**
2 eggs
almond essence

Pastry:
Place the flour and salt in a bowl and rub in the butter.
Add the potatoes and blend with a little water to form a stiff dough.
Roll out to line a 7 inch (18 cm) flan ring and cover the base with jam.
Prepare the filling by creaming the butter and sugar. Add the eggs and blend in the potatoes, almonds and essence.
Bake at 375°F (190°C), Gas Mark 5, for 45 minutes and dust with icing sugar.

Gilbert White of Selborne describes in fine detail the nest of a harvest mouse he found in a wheat field suspended in the head of a thistle, 'most artificially platted, and composed of blades of wheat, perfectly round, and about the size of a cricket ball; with the aperture so ingeniously closed, that there was no discovering to what part it belonged. It was so compact and well fitted that it would roll across the table without being discomposed, though it contained eight little mice that were naked and blind. As this nest was perfectly full, how could the dam come at her litter respectively so as to administer a teat to each? Perhaps she opens different places for the purpose, adjusting them again when the business is over; but she could not possibly be contained herself in the ball with her young, which moreover, would be daily increasing in bulk.'

Chocolate Potato Cake

3 oz [75 g] **mashed potatoes**
4 oz [125 g] **butter or margarine**
6 oz [150 g] **castor sugar**
2 eggs
6 oz [150 g] **self raising flour**
1½ oz [35 g] **melted chocolate** *or*
4 level teaspoons [4×5 ml spoons] **cocoa**
4 tablespoons [4×20 ml spoons] **milk**
½ level teaspoon [2.5 ml] **salt**

Cream the fat and sugar thoroughly with the mashed potato. If melted chocolate is used, add it to the creamed mixture.
Beat the eggs, and stir in.
Add the sifted dry ingredients and mix well.
Add the milk to make the mixture a soft, dropping consistency.
Divide the mixture evenly between two eight inch (20 cm) tins and bake in a moderate oven, 375°F (190°C), Gas Mark 5, for 25-30 minutes. Make sure it is quite firm and springy on top when pressed lightly.
Turn out on a rack to cool.
Sandwich together with any filling, then ice and decorate as desired. This cake keeps very well as the potato holds moisture and prevents it from drying out.

Coffee Nut Cookies

serves 4

3 oz [75 g] **cooked, sieved potato**
2 oz [50 g] **butter**
3 oz [75 g] **castor sugar**
1 egg
4 oz [100 g] **self raising flour**
2 oz [50 g] **desiccated coconut**
1 tablespoon [1×20 ml spoon]
liquid coffee

Cream together the butter and sugar.
Beat in the egg.
Stir in the dry ingredients, and the coffee.
Place small spoonfuls on a greased tin and bake at 400°F (200°C), Gas Mark 6, for 10-15 minutes.
For Coffee Nut Cake, add 1 tablespoon (1×20 ml spoon) milk to the recipe and bake at 350°F (180°C), Gas Mark 4, for 45 minutes.

Potato Doughnuts

serves 4

2 oz [50 g] **potatoes, sieved or riced**
4 oz [100 g] **plain flour**
1 rounded teaspoon [1×5 ml spoon] **baking powder**
2 oz [50 g] **butter**
1 egg, beaten
a pinch of cinnamon
castor sugar
deep fat
a pinch of salt

Sieve together the flour and baking powder.
Rub in the butter to resemble fine breadcrumbs.
Add 1 teaspoon (1×5 ml spoon) castor sugar, potatoes and cinnamon.
Bind together with the egg to form a stiff dough and roll out to about ½ inch (1 cm) thick on a floured board.
Stamp out rounds, removing the centre with a smaller cutter.
Deep fry for 5-7 minutes.
Drain and dredge with castor sugar.

Potato Cobbler

serves 4

8 oz [250 g] **cooked, sieved, potato**
1 lb [500 g] **rhubarb**
sugar to sweeten
8 oz [250 g] **self raising flour**
4 oz [100 g] **butter**
2 oz [50 g] **castor sugar**
a pinch of salt

Cut the rhubarb into pieces, wash well, and place in a pie dish with sugar to taste.
Place in the oven at 400°F (200°C), Gas Mark 6. This will be cooking while the topping is being made.
Rub the butter into sifted flour, salt and sugar.
Stir in the potato and knead together to form a dough.
Roll out on a lightly floured board, and cut into rounds.
Cover the hot fruit with the dough rounds, replace in the oven and continue baking for 15 minutes until cobbler is golden brown.
Dredge with castor sugar or icing sugar and serve hot.
Cooking time - 30 minutes.

Two gluttonous youngsters of
   Streatham
    Bought fifty-five doughnuts
   and eatham.
The coroner said,
   'No wonder they're dead;
How unwise of their parents to
   leatham!'

Potato Scone Whirls

serves 4

8 oz [250 g] **self raising flour**
6 oz [150 g] **cooked, sieved potato**
4 oz [100 g] **butter**
2 oz [50 g] **castor sugar**
milk to mix
a pinch of salt
Filling:
4 oz [100 g] **mixed dried fruit**
4 oz [100 g] **soft brown sugar**
½ level teaspoon [2.5 ml] **mixed spice**

Rub the butter into the flour, salt, sugar and potato.
Add the milk to bind the mixture.
Roll out to a rectangle.
Brush over with milk, and then cover with the filling well mixed together.
Roll up the dough, sealing the edges.
Cut into 12 pieces, and place cut side down on a greased baking sheet.
Bake at 450°F (230°C), Gas Mark 8, for 8-10 minutes.

Potato Apple Cake

serves 4

8 oz [250 g] **self raising flour**
4 oz [100 g] **cooked, sieved potato**
5 oz [150 g] **butter**
4 oz [100 g] **castor sugar**
a pinch of powdered cinnamon
2 large cooking apples
2 beaten eggs
a pinch of salt

Rub the butter into the sifted flour, salt and cinnamon.
Stir in the sugar, potato, and very thinly sliced apple.
Add the egg, and mix to a fairly soft consistency. If necessary, add a little cold milk.
Place the mixture in a greased loaf or cake tin, and bake at 375°F (190°C), Gas Mark 5, for 1-1½ hours.
Dredge with icing or castor sugar.

Potato Oatcakes

serves 4

1 lb [500 g] **potatoes, sieved or riced**
6 oz [150 g] **fine oatmeal**
a little milk to bind
salt

Mix together the potatoes, oatmeal and salt.
Add sufficient milk to form a stiff dough.
Roll out to about 1/8th inch (0.25 cm) thick on a floured board.
Prick with a fork and cut into rounds.
Bake quickly on a lightly greased heavy frying pan or griddle.
Serve with butter.
Ideal with soups or salads.

Steamed Date Pudding

serves 4

8 oz [250 g] **cooked, sieved potato**
3 oz [75 g] **chopped dates**
1 **beaten egg**
1 oz [25 g] **castor sugar**
2 oz [50 g] **melted butter**
grated rind of one orange
juice of one half orange
a pinch of salt

Mix together all the ingredients, adding more orange juice if necessary to make a soft consistency.
Pour the mixture into a lightly greased basin.
Cover, and steam for 1½ hours.
Serve, piping hot, with cream or a brandy sauce.

Traditional Potato Scones

serves 4

1 lb [500 g] **potatoes, sieved or riced**
4 oz [100 g] **plain flour**
butter
salt

Place all the ingredients in a bowl and knead well.
Roll out thinly, to about ⅛ inch (0.25 cm) thick, on a floured board.
Prick with a fork, and then cut into triangles.
Cook quickly in a lightly floured frying pan or on a griddle, browning on both sides.
Serve hot with butter.

The old English country squire was a paternal often eccentric character who played the leading part in the life of his neighbourhood and village. When he went to church he occupied his own special pew, often fitted out like a snug drawing room, with a fire, to be poked vigorously should the sermon go on too long. An amusing tale is told of Bishop Wilberforce when being shown a luxurious squire's pew, with a special fireplace, arm chairs, and 'every convenience'. When the clerk asked if the bishop could suggest any improvement, or the addition of any furniture, Wilberforce quietly whispered to the clergyman by his side, 'A card-table!'

Brompton Cake

serves 4

6 oz [150 g] **shortcrust pastry**
Filling:
8 oz [250 g] **potatoes, sieved or riced**
4 oz [100 g] **self raising flour**
3 oz [75 g] **castor sugar**
3 oz [75 g] **butter**
4 oz [100 g] **mixed dried fruit**

Line a greased 9 inch (23 cm) square tin with the pastry.
Cream butter and sugar together till it is light and fluffy.
Blend in the flour, potatoes, and dried fruit.
Place in the tin and bake at 350°F (180°C), Gas Mark 4, for 45 minutes. Use as a sweet, or a cake for tea.

Apple Balls

APPLE-TREE.

serves 4

12 oz [375 g] **potato pastry**
(**see page 22**)
4 **medium sized cooking apples**
2-3 **tablespoons** [2-3×20 ml
spoons] **marmalade**
2 oz [50 g] **currants**
1 oz [25 g] **butter**
1 oz [25 g] **granulated sugar**
a **few cloves**

Divide the pastry into four pieces,
and roll out each piece in a circle
large enough to cover each apple.
Peel and core the apples, leaving
whole.
Mix the marmalade and currants
with the butter which has been cut
into small pieces, and fill the
centre of the apple.
Cover the apple with the pastry,
seal at the top, and place in a
clove to form the stalk.
Bake at 425°F (220°C), Gas
Mark 7, for 15 minutes; turn
down heat to 350°F (180°C), Gas
Mark 4, and continue to bake for
approx. 30 minutes.
Remove from the oven and
sprinkle with coloured sugar.
To make coloured sugar:
Add one or two drops of red or
green colouring to approx. 1 oz
(25 g) granulated sugar.
Work with a teaspoon until
desired colour. Allow to dry.

Sunshine on apple trees on
Chritmas morning was believed to
lead to a fine crop of fruit in the
coming year. The strange custom
of wassailing the bare branches on
the eleventh day after Christmas
and firing on them with blank
cartridges was hoped to give more
positive encouragement for the
production of a bumper harvest.

Potato Wholemeal Bread

serves 4

8 oz [250 g] **potatoes, freshly boiled and sieved**
1½ lb [750 g] **100% wholemeal flour**
½ pint [250 ml] **potato water**
1 level dessertspoon [1×10 ml spoon] **sugar**
1 oz [25 g] **yeast**
3 level teaspoons [3×5 ml spoons] **salt**

Mix the potatoes, hot water and sugar in a bowl, stirring until well blended.
Allow to cool to lukewarm.
Crumble in the yeast, mix and leave in a warm place for 10 minutes.
Add the flour and salt gradually to make a soft dough that does not stick to the bowl or hands. Knead until smooth and elastic.
Place in a large bowl, cover with a clean cloth and put in a warm place to rise until double its size.
Knead again and shape into two loaves.
Place in greased tins, cover and leave to rise until double the bulk.
Bake at 450°F (230°C), Gas Mark 8, for 15 minutes.
Reduce the heat to 375°F (190°C), Gas Mark 5, and bake for 30-45 minutes until the bread gives a hollow sound when tapped on the bottom.

Pommes Savoyarde

serves 4

1 lb [500 g] **potatoes**
2 **onions**
4 or 5 **rashers bacon**
2 oz [50 g] **Cheddar cheese, grated**
½ pint [250 ml] **stock**
1 oz [25 g] **butter**
salt and pepper

Dice the bacon and fry lightly in the butter.
Remove from the pan and fry the sliced onion.
Peel and slice the potatoes, and toss in the same fat with the onion.
Add the bacon, stock and seasoning to taste.
Turn into an ovenproof dish and cover with the cheese.
Bake at 375°F (190°C), Gas Mark 5, for about an hour, until the potatoes are tender.

Pommes au Lard

serves 4

1½ lb [750 g] **potatoes**
4 oz [100 g] **bacon rashers**
4 oz [100 g] **onion, chopped**
stock
salt and pepper

Peel and cut the potatoes into quarters. Dice the bacon.
Place the potatoes, bacon and onion in a pan, just cover with stock, and season to taste.
Simmer gently until the potatoes are tender.
Garnish with chopped parsley.

Pommes Gaufrette

serves 4

Choose medium sized potatoes.
Slice on a mandolin, giving a half turn with the wrist each time. This gives a lattice effect on the potato.
Fry as for game chips.

Pommes Parisienne

serves 4

1 lb [500 g] **large potatoes, peeled**
2 oz [50 g] **butter**
salt

Using a vegetable scoop spoon, scoop out potatoes into small balls and parboil.
Sauté lightly in butter until golden brown.

Pommes Macaire

serves 4

4 **potatoes, baked**
2 oz [50 g] **butter**
salt and pepper
fat for frying

Bake jacket potatoes.
Scoop out pulp and mash with a fork.
Add butter and seasoning.
Shape into large medallions and shallow fry on both sides until golden brown.

Pommes Boulangère

serves 4

1 lb [500 g] **potatoes**
2 good sized onions
½ pint [250 ml] **good stock**
1 oz [25 g] **butter**
salt and pepper

Slice the onions and cook in butter until they are transparent.
Peel and slice the potatoes, place in an ovenproof dish together with the onions and sprinkle with salt and pepper.
Add the stock and the butter and bake for about an hour at 375°F (190°C), Gas Mark 5.

Pommes Allumettes

serves 4

1 lb [500 g] **medium sized potatoes, peeled**
oil
salt

Cut the potatoes into very thin strips like matchsticks and leave to soak in cold water to remove excess starch.
Drain off the water and dry the potatoes thoroughly in a clean, dry tea towel.
Fry in deep fat until crisp and golden brown.
Drain on absorbent kitchen paper and serve hot sprinkled with salt.

Pommes Gratinées

serves 4

1 lb [500 g] **potatoes, cooked and sieved**
1 oz [25 g] **butter**
4 oz [100 g] **Cheddar cheese, grated**
some browned breadcrumbs
salt and pepper

Mix together the hot potato, butter, a little cheese, and seasoning to taste.
Spread in a buttered gratin dish and cover with the remaining cheese and breadcrumbs.
Grill until the cheese is golden brown.

Many superstitions are connected with the prediction of weather. For example, stepping on a spider or a black beetle brings about rain; while cobwebs patterning the grass in the early morning means that a fine day lies ahead.

Pommes Delmonico

serves 4

1 lb [500 g] **potatoes cut into**
   ½ in [1 cm] cubes
a pinch of grated nutmeg
1 oz [25 g] butter
milk
breadcrumbs
salt and pepper

Place cubed potatoes into a pan
with salt, pepper, nutmeg and
½ oz (12.5 g) butter.
Add sufficient milk to cover and
cook until just tender. Leave lid
off pan while cooking.
Place in a greased casserole,
sprinkle with breadcrumbs and
dot with remaining butter.
Brown under a hot grill.

Potato Wine

Take ½ gallon of small potatoes,
wash them well and cut them in
half. Put them into a pan with 1
gallon of fresh cold water with 3
pieces of root ginger, bring to the
boil, boil for 10 minutes.

Have another pan ready, into
which you have put 3 lbs. of
granulated sugar and 2 sliced
oranges and 2 sliced lemons.
Strain the potato water on to the
sugar, etc., and boil again for ½
hour. When cold, bottle, and as
soon as the wine has finished
working, cork tightly. No yeast is
required.

Recipe reprinted
from Farmhouse Fare

Pommes Dauphine

serves 4

1 lb [500 g] duchesse potatoes
8 oz [250 g] choux pastry
choux pastry recipe:
2½ oz [60 g] plain flour
2 eggs
¼ pint [125 ml] water
1½ oz [37 g] butter
oil
salt

Place the butter and water in a
saucepan and bring to the boil.
Remove from the heat, add the
flour and beat well.
Allow the mixture to cool, add the
eggs and salt and beat
thoroughly. Add to duchesse
potatoes, blending well.
Form into cork shapes 2 inches
(5 cm) in length and fry in deep,
hot oil until golden brown.

Pommes Duchesse

serves 4

1 lb [500 g] boiled potatoes
   sieved or riced
1 oz [25 g] butter
1 egg, beaten
salt and pepper

Add the egg, butter and seasoning
to the potatoes and beat
thoroughly.
This mixture can be piped into
pyramids and also as instructed in
recipes.

Pommes Anna

serves 4

1½ lb [750 g] potatoes
4 oz [100 g] butter
salt and pepper

Peel and cut the potatoes into thin
slices.
Wash and dry them thoroughly.
Butter a shallow ovenproof dish
and cover the base with
overlapping potato slices. Season
well and pour over a little melted
butter.
Continue with similar layers of
potato, seasoning and butter.
Cover the dish and bake for ¾-1
hour at 400°F (200°C), Gas
Mark 6.
Turn out the potato mould,
serve hot cut in wedges like a
cake.
Drain off excess butter to be used
another time.
If Pommes Anna are to be a
garnish, fill dariole moulds and
bake for about 30 minutes.

Elderberry Wine

Take 7 lbs. berries and 2 gallons of water. To each gallon of liquid add 3 lbs. best loaf sugar, 1 lb. raisins, ½ oz. ground ginger, ½ oz. whole ginger, bruised, 6 cloves, ½ stick cinnamon.

Strip the berries from the stalks; pour boiling water over them. Let them stand for 24 hours, then bruise them well and strain through a hair sieve or jelly-bag. Measure the liquid, put into an earthenware pan and add sugar and a lemon cut in slices. Boil the cloves, ginger, raisins and cinnamon in a little of the liquid. Strain and add to the rest of the wine.

Allow to stand for a few days, then take off the cap. Strain again and pour into stone jars or casks. Leave open for a few weeks, continually adding more wine until fermentation ceases. Bung tightly and let it remain for 6 months, then bottle.

Recipe reprinted from Farmhouse Fare